The Nabobs at Home

By the same author

High Noon of Empire
Indian Temples and Palaces
A Season in Hell,
the defence of the Lucknow Residency
The Myth of the Mahatma
The Sahibs and the Lotus

THE
NABOBS
AT HOME

Michael Edwardes

CONSTABLE · LONDON

First published in Great Britain 1991
by Constable and Company Limited
3 The Lanchesters, 162 Fulham Palace Road
London W6 9ER
Copyright © 1991 by Michael Edwardes
The right of Michael Edwardes to be
identified as the author of this Work
has been asserted by him in accordance
with the Copyright, Designs & Patents Act 1988
ISBN 0 09 469120 7
Set in Monophoto 12pt Sabon by
Servis Filmsetting Limited, Manchester
Printed in Great Britain by
St Edmundsbury Press Limited
Bury St Edmunds, Suffolk

A CIP catalogue record for this book
is available from the British Library

*For Rosemary and Jean Spacek, in whose
houses this book was written*

General Clive has arrived, all over estates
and diamonds.

H. Walpole to H. Mann, 23 March 1758

In such a revolution (in Bengal) it was
impossible but that a number of
individuals should have acquired large
property. They did acquire it; and with it
seem to have obtained the detestation of
their countrymen, and the appellation of
nabob as a term of reproach.

Price's Tracts i, 13 (1777)

Contents

Illustrations

The Nabob
or
Asiatic Plunderer

IN the second half of the eighteenth century, the British upper classes felt, and displayed, both publicly and privately, the sort of panic that might have been caused by the arrival in England of the hordes of Genghiz Khan – carrying the plague. The actual invasion was that of a comparatively small number of men who had acquired, by various means, usually dubious, large fortunes in India which they intended to spend in ensuring their entry into 'society'. That is to say, into the political, social, and economic preserves of the English landed gentry.

The opposition to these men – they were quickly named 'nabobs' after *nawab*, the Indian word for an Indian Muslim prince – took various forms. Satirical literature – the title of this chapter is that of a play by Samuel Foote, first published in 1773; satirical drawings – cartoons by such men as Rowlandson and Gillray; satirical remarks, laced with venom, in Parliament, the salon, and, most vicious of all, in private correspondence and journals. Horace Walpole, wit, gothic novelist and son of Britain's first true prime minister, wrote in a letter to a friend that the 'nabobs' had starved 'millions by monopolies and plunder' in India and now threatened to create a 'famine at home by the luxury occasioned by their opulence raising the price of everything, till the poor could not purchase bread'. An exaggeration that demonstrates Walpole's fear and distaste more than any real threat to the standard of living of the lower classes.

Some saw the 'nabobs' as figures of fun, who:

Rich in everything but sense
Display their haughty dull magnificence.

Others, however, were outraged. 'Without connections, without any natural interest in the soil, the importers of foreign gold have forced their way into Parliament by such a torrent of corruption, as no private hereditary fortune can resist.' And that was from the Earl of Chatham, at one time known as the 'Great Commoner', whose brilliant political career had been made possible by the acumen of his grandfather, Thomas Pitt, in acquiring, when Governor of Madras, the famous stone known as the Pitt Diamond, in a manner that would hardly survive serious scrutiny. Respectability is, of course, often a matter of time, the years that have elapsed since one's ancestor slept with a king or another acquired a fortune by what can only be described as a confidence trick. The descendants are frequently *plus royaliste que le roi*, if only in defence of what they have become.

It was not only among the aristocracy that criticism thrived. Dr Samuel Johnson, responding to an assertion by his biographer, James Boswell, that a nabob would not carry an election to Parliament from a man of family, despite the decay of respect for such people, replied: 'Why, sir, the nabob will carry it by means of his wealth, in a country where money is highly valued, as it must be where nothing can be had without money.' But, of course, his preference was for 'men of family'.

What sort of people were those who could incite both fear and loathing not only in members of the Establishment, but in such prickly outsiders as the same Dr Johnson, who could assert that 'there are few ways in which a man can be more innocently employed than in getting money'? Very few of the Doctor's contemporaries were prepared to accept that the nabobs had acquired their wealth by legitimate means. But where had they acquired it, and how? In effect, what made a nabob?

2

The Land of the Pagoda Tree
or
The Making of a Nabob

Most of those whose riches seemed to threaten the established order of things in Britain made their fortunes in Bengal during the twenty-seven years between 1757 and 1784. Though there were some soldiers among them, they were mainly merchants, traders, who became kingmakers, masters of Bengal, the founders, in fact, of the British empire in India.

No thoughts of dominion troubled the minds of the first British merchants in India early in the seventeenth century. They went there for gain, both corporate and individual. Most of the merchants were employed by the English East India Company established in 1601 to enjoy some of the profits of the trade in spices, silks, gems, and other luxuries of the Gorgeous East, up until then monopolized by the Portuguese and the Dutch. On their arrival on the west coast, the English merchants found that most of India was ruled by the Mughals, as Muslim dynasty founded in 1526 by a direct descendant of Tamerlane and Genghiz Khan. His great grandson, Jehangir, gave them permission to establish a trading post and, finally, in 1612 the Company set up warehouses at Surat, then the chief port of western India.

The British had their first contact with Bengal in the 1630s after they had received permission to set up a trading post there.

Growing trade produced friction between the merchants and local officials over the amount of customs and other duties. Protracted negotiations were interrupted in 1686 when the Company's agent, Job Charnock, declared war against the might of the Mughal empire. The Company's ten ships and 600 men – all that was available in the area – proved inadequate to the task, and the British were forced to abandon their posts and flee to Madras. In spite of the disastrous failure of what was in fact an attempted coup, the merchants were able to negotiate a treaty, and in 1690 the Company's ships were once again moored in the Hugli river, near a spot where they founded what was to become the capital of British India. In 1696 the British were given leave to fortify Calcutta, and a fort – named in 1699 Fort William after the Dutch King of England – was erected. In the same year, three nearby villages were purchased. The Company had become an Indian landowner.

As the new century dawned, the British could look at their Indian activities with a certain amount of satisfaction. Their trading posts at Bombay on the west coast, Madras and Cuddalore on the south east, and now Calcutta in Bengal, were thriving towns and the volume of trade was increasing steadily. In the past, the Company had had its good times and its bad. In England, its wealth had been looked upon with envy by both king and Parliament, and the Company had suffered. Economic rivalry, encouraged by political factions, lasted until 1708, when the Company amalgamated with its principal competitor. In India, there remained the other Europeans. The Portuguese were in irreversible decline, the Dutch were still powerful, but the real threat was to come from a late arrival in India, the French. Indeed, it soon became clear that the French were not just concerned with trade.

The clue to this enlarged ambition lay in the state of India itself. The Mughal empire, whose wealth and splendour had first attracted the Europeans, at the end of the eighteenth century was riven by subversion. First established by an alien Muslim minority, it was then ruled by a collaboration between that minority and indigenous Hindu princes. But the rigidly Muslim emperor Aurangzeb, who ascended to the throne in 1659, created a climate favourable to rebellion. By the time of his death in 1707 the empire was ready to fall apart.

Aurangzeb's successor managed to maintain the central authority of the empire, but after his death, a mere five years later, palace revolution followed palace revolution in the Mughal capital of Delhi. The great nobles and provincial governors began to look to their own independent future. They followed the example of the greatest of them all, the governor of the Deccan, who, in 1723, set himself up as the ruler of this vast segment of southern central India. But he had to contend for his independence with the Marathas, a hardy race of Hindu cultivators from western India who had appeared on the stage, late in the seventeenth century, conscious, it seemed, only of the present and unencumbered by the past – for historically they emerged from nowhere – to threaten the empire. In 1738 the Marathas reached and plundered the outer suburbs of the imperial capital and gained from the then Mughal emperor the province of Malwa, which effectively divided the northern part of the empire from the Deccan. Within the next few years their territories lay within a few miles of the British in Bombay, and one of their number had set himself up as the raja of a state near the British settlement of Cuddalore. Later, driving eastwards towards the Bay of Bengal, they even attacked some of the Company's shipping on the river Hugli.

The Mughal empire had also to contend with foreign invasions. In 1739, the Persian king Nadir Shah sacked Delhi and then withdrew with the loot. For a while, there was a last efflorescence of Mughal power, but it died with the emperor Muhammed Shah in 1748. New invasions, this time by the Afghans, crushed the central authority of the empire. The loosening of restraints and the release of ambitions were most strongly felt in the south, where the Mughal power had always been at its weakest. Unlike the Marathas, who seemed to be self-sufficient, the contenders in the south were too evenly matched. They needed allies, and it was the French who first saw the possibilities that lay in helping the winning side.

The French had been trading in India since 1668, and most of their trading stations were near those of the British. Their headquarters, Pondicherry, was some eighty-five miles south of Madras. At first, the relations between the two Companies were, if not cordial, at least tolerant. During the war of the Spanish Succession (1702–13), involving Britain and France in Europe, the two Companies kept an unofficial truce. But when war broke out in Europe again in 1740, no truce could be arranged, and in 1746, the French captured Madras, only to be forced to return it after peace was signed two years later. The conflict revealed not only the weakness of the British in the south, but the prizes that lay to be grasped by French intervention in Indian politics.

In 1748 Dupleix, the governor of Pondicherry, began to play Indian politics with great skill and daring. In that year the ruler of the Deccan died, and his death was followed by conflict among his heirs. The territories that touched upon the European settlements in the south were ruled by a subordinate known as the nawab of the Carnatic. The French backed a brilliant contender, Chanda Sahib; and with the aid of a few hundred French troops he was placed in power and his predecessor killed. Also assassinated was the new ruler of the Deccan, and a French force put a French nominee on his empty throne. In return the new ruler declared Dupleix governor of all south India below the river Kistna.

The British had no doubt about the Frenchman's real target. Dupleix was not out for territorial dominion but for a monopoly of trade. The British had to fight, and as they were nominally at peace with France, through Indian surrogates. They recognized another contender as nawab of the Carnatic, one Muhammad Ali, son of the man killed by the French. The British also began to train Indian soldiers in the European fashion and to stiffen them with European troops and artillery. As commander they had one good professional, Stringer Lawrence, and one brilliant amateur, Robert Clive, who had originally come out to India as a clerk. The British were successful in placing their man as ruler of the Carnatic, but the French still remained a powerful force in the Deccan and had no obvious intention of giving up any of their ambitions.

In the south, the British soon assessed – and collected – the very real profits of intervention in Indian affairs. In Bengal, however, the situation was somewhat different. The ruler, Nawab Alivardi Khan, nominally still an official of the empire, but in fact independent, was strong enough to overawe the Europeans and keep their enmities under control. But he could not destroy their ambitions, nor the casual and unthinking arrogance that so often partnered them. The Europeans believed their time would come. Alivardi Khan would not live for ever. Indeed, he did not, dying at the ripe age of eighty-two in April 1756.

To everyone's surprise, the chosen heir, Siraj-ud-daulah, succeeded to the throne without opposition. One Englishman described the new nawab as 'violent, passionate, of great ambition tinctured with avarice'. And it seems, though there is no hard evidence, that the British had deliberately offended him by supporting other rivals to the throne. They had also, rather foolishly, given protection, not only to his enemies, but to men whose wealth he had intended to expropriate.

The lessons of French and British activity in southern India had not been lost on the new nawab, and he was determined to keep the Europeans in his territory as much under control as his predecessor had done. When he learned that both the French and the British were fortifying their settlements, he ordered them to stop. The French obeyed; the British not only did not, but also treated the nawab's envoy with insolent contempt. No one was more surprised than the arrogant merchants of Calcutta when in May 1756, the nawab demanded that the fortifications be razed and that the trading rights held by the British should end.

The nawab's first overt act against the British was not at Calcutta, but at Kasimbazar, a trading station near to the nawab's capital of Murshidabad, a city as large as contemporary London. As the fort at Kasimbazar was indefensible – the earthworks had been undermined by rats – the place was soon captured. The next to fall was Calcutta. It must have seemed to the nawab that the British had been severely chastised for their arrogance. But he had not sufficiently appreciated what had been happening in south India. By 1756, the British there had built up substantial forces to fight their wars against the French, and were able to send a fleet from Madras under the command of Admiral Watson, and with troops led by Robert Clive. They arrived in the Hugli river early in December, 1756.

The campaign that followed was not a pleasant one but it was certainly successful for, on 2 January 1757, Calcutta was retaken and its safety secured by the capture of another town a few miles up river. Calcutta lay in ruins, but there was no real point in starting the task of reconstruction until the situation was a little clearer. The new arrivals were put into hastily erected huts while Clive and Watson considered what to do next. There had to be negotiations with the nawab; but what about the French, who had been sitting in their trading station at Chandernagar some twenty miles up river from Calcutta, quietly rejoicing at the plight of the British? The French were still very much a power in the Deccan. Would the commander there move on Bengal to help his compatriots seize another opportunity, or even more threatening, on Madras, as the place had been denuded of troops to send to Bengal?

It was a time of decision. Clive sent envoys to the nawab who had, with reluctance, accepted what was the end of hostilities. At the nawab's capital there were layers of intrigue like a palimpsest. The French had an envoy there, and there was no shortage of potential conspirators among the Indians. The trouble was that no one could really be sure who was conspiring with whom and for what precise end. Factions were rife and ever changing. The nawab could not make up his mind between the French and the British. Clive helped to resolve the situation by marching from Calcutta and on 20 March, seizing the French settlement at Chandernagar.

It was a decisive act in an anarchy of indecision. It helped to crystallize a conspiracy. Its principals were Mir Jafar, one of the nawab's ministers, Rai Durlabh, a Hindu whose authority was being undermined; the most important financial power in northern India, known by the title of Jagat Seth, 'banker of the world', given to him by one of the less transient of recent Mughal emperors; another Hindu banker, Omichund; and Nand Kumar, governor of Hugli, a double-agent, prudently – though in the long run not prudently enough – backing all sides and taking bribes from most. It was a conspiracy of strength: Jagat Seth held the purse strings, Mir Jafar as commander in chief, the army; the others knew their way about the labyrinths of profitable intrigue. And there were others, openly and without reservation, pro-British. For Clive it was an irresistible combination.

Clive's agent, William Watts, hidden in a palanquin normally used to carry women, met Mir Jafar in the latter's zenana, and there a treaty was concluded: Mir Jafar would be the next nawab and the British his loyal beneficiaries. By the treaty, the Company was to be given large grants of land and restitution for its financial losses, and most of the Company's employees were promised substantial sums of money for their sufferings and services. It only remained to overthrow the nawab. This was done, without much assistance from the conspirators, by Clive at what was little more than a skirmish at Plassey on 23 June 1757. Within a week, the nawab, Siraj-ud-daula, was dead, murdered by Mir Jafar's son. The new nawab, placed on the throne by Robert Clive, rewarded those who had put him there. Unfortunately, the late nawab's treasury turned out to be less full than had been expected. Nevertheless, it was a time of almost universal profit – at least among the British. Where once they had been merely traders, they were now the makers of kings and received their just rewards.

Clive described the consequences of Plassey and the intrigues of which it was merely the tip of the iceberg, as 'this great revolution so happily brought about'. What he meant was the complete reversal of the fortunes of the British. His intentions and those of his colleagues were to do little more than re-establish the Company's trade in Bengal on a preferential footing, and to ensure that such preference would be maintained by the nawab. In actual fact, the events of 1757 had created a climate of continual revolution, for they had irrevocably undermined the authority of the nawab. It was certain that if the new nawab failed to live up to expectations, the British would once again intervene. Clive's successors thought they needed a new nawab, and this was easily accomplished in 1760.

Three years after they had placed their own man on the throne, the British found that he too was unsatisfactory. The new nawab, Mir Kasim, was undoubtedly determined to protect his authority from fresh British interventions. The British responded by declaring war on Mir Kasim, and restoring the man he had replaced to the throne of Bengal. This time, the revolution was neither bloodless nor smooth. Mir Kasim did not wait for the British to arrest him. Moving towards the eastern borders of Bengal, he executed those British he could lay his hands on as well as some of the more prominent of their Indian allies. Finally, he joined up with the ruler of the neighbouring state of Oudh and the Mughal emperor, Shah Alam, then a fugitive from his own capital of Delhi. This coalition could well have overwhelmed the British had the latter's military com-manders been as inept as their civilian leaders. Encountering the enemy at Buxar, a spot halfway between Patna and Banaras, the British defeated them in a hard fought and bloody battle on 24 October 1764. One of the consequences of the state of affairs in Bengal was the return to India of Robert Clive, principally with the task of cleaning out corruption from the Company's administration, a classic example of turning the poacher into the gamekeeper. Clive and his friends had been able to use Mir Kasim's massacre of the Englishmen for their own purposes, and had seized control of the Company in London. They in turn gave Clive almost complete freedom of action.

Clive moved through Bengal like a whirlwind. Every employee of the Company was compelled to sign a covenant prohibiting him from accepting 'presents' or engaging in private trade. The army, which became restive after Clive's abolition of certain over-generous allowances, was firmly disciplined. A new, young, and totally subservient nawab was placed on the throne of Bengal, and peace was made with the emperor Shah Alam, who in return granted the British the legal authority to rule Bengal. For this, Clive promised to pay a regular subsidy, but he was no longer of the opinion that the British could or should put the emperor back on his throne. They were not yet ready for such an imperial role. Nor were they ready to take over direct control of the government of Bengal. There were just not enough men who could be trusted not to take advantage of their positions. The administration remained Indian in law and method, though real power lay still with the British – and everyone who mattered knew it.

Clive's actions against private trade and other privileges were accompanied by a display of moral indignation which inflamed the raw wounds of his victims. Before Clive returned to England in July 1767, he had hurt a lot of people in their most vulnerable part – their pockets – and they were to have their revenge.

In Bengal, fortunes were still being made, many of them at the expense of the Company, whose revenues declined to such a state that in 1772 it was forced to seek a loan from the British government. It got its money, and also, and less acceptable, an Act of Parliament 'establishing certain regulations for the better management of the affairs of the East India Company, as well as India as in Europe'. Among the many provisions of the new Act was that anyone 'employed or concerned in the collection of the revenues, or the administration of justice' was forbidden to engage in private trade. Others could still trade, and there were always methods by which any regulation could be circumvented, but the Act did make a start on bringing to an end a period in which trading fortunes had been made through the abuse of power. 'We are men of power,' wrote one who exercised it, 'and take advantage of it. Why, . . . what is the use of station if we are not to benefit from it?' There is plenty of evidence of the use of violence and intimidation, especially by the Indian agents of European traders. But the idea that the rapacity of the British somehow sucked dry the economy of Bengal is mainly an invention of the enemies of the 'nabobs', perpetuated by later historians of British India. The economy of Bengal was too vast and diverse to be controlled by a small band of foreigners. Still, even under the Regulating Act there were profits to be gained by one means or another, until another Act, that of 1784, ushered in a new order for British India.

Clive's triumph at Plassey and its consequences opened up a golden age of corruption and bribery to the British in Bengal. The taking of 'presents' was nothing new to them, nor was the exploitation of authority for profit, but Plassey released opportunities undreamed of before. In 1772 a committee of the House of Commons listed over £2m taken in presents between 1757 and 1765, an enormous sum in the values of the time.

Mir Jafar, as soon as he had been secured upon his throne, was obliged to pay those who had put him there. Out of the sums dispersed Clive received about £234,000, the new nawab expressing himself to Clive that 'I had been one of the principal means of not only getting him the throne, but of saving his life'.

Others received sums ranging from over £80,000 down to a subaltern in the army at £3,000. Half the presents were paid immediately in gold and silver, or in jewels with a promise to pay the remainder over three years. Clive was, however, not satisfied, and eighteen months after Plassey he asked for a *jagir* or grant of revenue, to support the title of *Zubdat ul Mulk* (Select of the State), which Mir Jafar had obtained for him from the emperor Shah Alam. An ingenious scheme was worked out by the nawab's bankers, by which Clive received a *jagir* worth about £27,000 a year, but which was secured on lands that had been leased to the Company by the nawab! This meant that Clive became the Company's landlord. The Company agreed to this, but soon regretted its decision. His enemies even persuaded the Company to cancel the grant, but they ultimately allowed him to draw from the revenues of Bengal £27,000 a year for life.

Clive felt it necessary – as indeed it was – to prepare a defence for the taking of presents. It was one to be used over and over again by others. If such presents were offered freely for real services done in the course of duty, but in no way affecting the Company's interest, he claimed then they should be allowed. If they tended to corrupt or were the result of menaces, then they were not permissible. An unsolicited gift was a mark of honour rather than anything else. Clive insisted he had never brought pressure to bear on Mir Jafar. The 'revolution' he had engineered was for the interests of the Company and Britain. The rest were fringe benefits.

Actually, the payments were the results of a meeting of two desires. Mir Jafar wanted to be nawab, and was prepared to pay for it. Clive was ready to assist him, and was willing to be paid for his services. It was really a very simple formula – and easily replicated. After Clive's departure, and the replacement of Mir Jafar by Mir Kasim, more presents were given, amounting in all to about £225,000. Of course, Clive's justification for the taking of presents was invoked this time. The 'presents' were voluntary, and nobody had asked Mir Kasim for anything. The exact facts of the matter are not identifiable, but if money had not been bargained for, it was certainly accepted. Mir Kasim, like his predecessors, was not merely showing gratitude. He was buying his future. And everybody knew it.

After the defeat of Mir Kasim and the reinstatement of Mir Jafar, a bill was presented covering a wide variety of 'services'. Payment of about £500,000 was negotiated. On the death of Mir Jafar in February 1765, despite the fact that an instruction from the Directors of the Company forbidding the acceptance of presents had arrived in January, payments were extracted from the new nawab and his ministers. Compared to other sums, the total was quite modest, amounting only to about £112,000.

The bonanza years of 1757–1765 were not to be repeated. The ability of the nawabs of Bengal to pay was considerably reduced over the years. The nawabs had become pensioners on an annuity from the Company, with less and less available for distribution as 'presents'. But as the Company's military power spread outwards from Bengal, other Indian rulers began to recognize the advantages of purchasing the goodwill and services of Company officials. As the Company established diplomatic relations with Indian courts, and appointed Residents at their capitals, such appointments became very lucrative. But the accepting of presents was subject to too much risk after the provisions of the Regulating Act of 1772 were enforced. It was very difficult, if not impossible, to hide a large present successfully. But if large presents were becoming a thing of the past, there still remained a wide range of perquisites and other sources of private profit, such as extortion or fraud. Revenue farming was often practised where sums were either embezzled directly, or an extra tax imposed for the benefit of the 'farmer'.

Among the many frauds on the Company, the worst were concerned with military buildings. After Plassey, a great new fort was built at Calcutta. Very large sums were paid out to non-existent workers, and materials were charged with a mark-up exceeding 50 per cent. Calcutta was by no means an isolated example. Matters were worse in the dependent states, such as Oudh or Banaras. In the latter, the first Resident, appointed in 1764, took over the mint and creamed off a percentage of the revenue. As for Oudh, its capital Lucknow, wrote the governor-general, Warren Hastings, was a 'sink of iniquity . . . the school of rapacity'. There 'beardless boys' were able to gamble £20,000 at a sitting, all acquired from the 'generosity' of the ruler.

The eighteenth century held a somewhat flexible view on the standards of morality of the man in office. It did not countenance embezzlement and fraud. If the Company had only had the means of detecting such crimes, there is no doubt that many of the Company's employees in all ranks would have been prosecuted. One of the obstacles to such action was the Company's slowness in deciding just what practices were unacceptable to it. The net had too many holes, and a great number of fish both big and small escaped through them.

Once they had made their fortune, the merchant, administrator and soldier were anxious to quit India as quickly as possible so that they might live the life of a gentleman back home. Few enjoyed living in India, though they could do so with an extravagance and opulent display they would never be able to exercise at home. Most of the British, however, disliked India, hating the climate, the disease and 'the blacks'. The ambitions of the majority were on the whole modest: a house in the country with some land and a comfortable income from the estate or from savings in Government Stock. But for some, ambitions ran higher, and especially so after Plassey. Now, a man newly retired from Bengal wanted a great mansion, a string of estates, and political influence. Clive was the role-model for them.

The fulfilment of such ambitions, whether modest or grand, faced similar obstacles. For one thing, there was a less than fifty-fifty chance of getting back to Britain to enjoy one's hard-earned fortune. Between 1757 and 1766, 59 per cent of the Company's employees died in India. That was, in fact, an improvement on the period 1747 to 1756, when the figure had been 74 per cent! With the influx of larger numbers after Plassey, the figure dropped to 44 per cent.

Perhaps the greatest enemy – for if it did not kill of itself, it opened the body to, and then intensified, the effect of other diseases – was intemperance. With vast quantities of food usually consumed at the hottest time of the day, went enormous amounts of wines and liquors. The description of one dinner party, at which a party of fourteen drank forty-two bottles of claret, and a similar quantity of Madeira, was not unusual. No wonder liver complaints were commonplace. Dr John Lind, the physician who published a learned *Essay on Diseases* in 1768, considered Bengal one of the most unhealthy places in the world, and found that part of India fitted his criteria perfectly, for it had 'thick and noisome fogs, swarms of flies, corruption of butcher's meat, and a sandy soil'. He strongly advised staying indoors on a foggy night, and to protect against the sun, 'a bladder dipped in vinegar'. In particularly unhealthy spots, he recommended that a man should 'chew rhubarb, stop his nose with linen dipped in camphor and vinegar, and drink a concoction of bark, garlic, and rhubarb in brandy'. By 'bark', the learned doctor meant quinine, which had been known in India as a specific against fever since the early part of the eighteenth century. On the whole, most medical treatments were ineffective and, not infrequently, made matters worse. The most certain way of keeping healthy and surviving India in order to live comfortably in England was exercise and a regulated diet. One of those who followed such a regimen, Warren Hastings, rode eight miles before breakfast and then had a cold bath. He drank nothing stronger than tea or water, never ate supper, and went to bed at ten.

Assuming then, that a man survived the vicissitudes of life in India, there was still one more obstacle to be surmounted. He had to get his fortune back to England. Some of it, of course, could be left behind in India, but it was a very dangerous thing to confide money to Indian bankers, merchants, or even Europeans, without personal supervision. One method available to planters in the West Indies, for example, was to invest money in goods to be shipped on their behalf to London and there sold. In India, however, such was forbidden because the East India Company controlled the monopoly of trade from India, and would not permit a British subject to ship goods on his own account to Europe. But every monopoly has its exception. The Company *did* allow limited concessions for private trade in its ships. This privilege was, on the whole, granted only to the captains and other officers of the Company's own vessels, though most of them were willing to sell the privilege at a price.

One commodity the Company did not deal in was precious stones. These it was prepared to carry on its ships for a customs fee. Unfortunately, both the supply of stones and their price fluctuated. After Plassey, the capability of the Indian diamond mines to supply the demand fell short. Robert Clive found in 1765 that 'diamonds were not to be had; the sums of money sent out and private fortunes demand ten times the quantity'. Still, where there is a demand somehow there is always a supply, and when the British found themselves at Banaras, the centre of the diamond trade in northern India, they were quick to take advantage of it.

Another way of remitting money to Britain was through a bill of exchange. The Company allowed its representatives in India to accept money from individuals in return for bills of exchange redeemable in London at rates fixed by the Company. The Company thus acquired ready cash for its activities in India. In return, the purchaser of a bill of exchange was guaranteed their payment. There were, however, a few disadvantages, one of the most important being public disclosure. The sums involved could not be kept secret. Another disadvantage was that the Company placed stringent limits on the sums that could be transmitted in this manner.

Of course, there were other means of transmission. The Portuguese, the Dutch, the French, even the Danes, the Holy Roman Empire, and other European companies would accept money against bills. It was suggested that it was illegal for a British subject in India to do such a thing, but the matter was not made absolutely so until an Act of Parliament of 1781. After Plassey, the Company found itself unable to accommodate the demand for bills of exchange, and those with money turned, inevitably, to foreigners, Clive among them, using the Dutch as transmitters. Even the French were used, showing as always, that money has no nationality or even a great deal of patriotism.

When Robert Clive left Bengal in 1760, he took with him the then largest fortune ever made by one man in India. £230,000 of it was in Dutch bills, £30,000 in diamonds, £41,000 in bills on the Company, £4000 on certificates on East India Company ships, £5000 on Bombay and £7000 in the form of a bill of exchange drawn on one of the Directors of the Company, Lawrence Sulivan. There was also the income from Clive's *jagir* of £27,000 per annum. The two years of his return (1765–7) produced a remittance of £165,000 though there were no presents or profits from private trade.

The sums transmitted by Clive were unique, but lesser persons were also able to send home substantial sums. One James Johnstone, a member of the Bengal council, who had singlemindedly and with considerable ruthlessness sought a fortune, was supposed to have been worth around £300,000 when he returned to Scotland, there to purchase three estates and considerable parliamentary interest. Johnstone had very sensibly taken himself back to Britain before Clive arrived in India for the second time. Among the military perhaps the most conspicuous of those who made a fortune was Richard Smith, who when he left Bengal after a stay of six years and rising to the rank of commander-in-chief was said to be worth between £200,000 and £300,000.

It was around this time that it was suggested that in India, and in particular in Bengal, there grew a money tree, an exotic tree, of course, as befitted an exotic land, a *pagoda-tree*, so-called after the gold coin of the same name, that could be shaken and money picked up off the ground. It must well have seemed that money grew on trees, both to those who had made their fortune after

Plassey and to those who envied and feared them. Fear and envy are prime inspirations for caricature, and the men who had made their fortune in Bengal were often viciously caricatured, but what sort of men were they? The 'savage old nabob with an immense fortune, a tawny complexion, a bad liver and a worse heart' of T.B. Macaulay? Or the courteous, cultured Warren Hastings, one of the founders of Oriental scholarship?

The nabobs were certainly not barbarians, nor on the whole men who had emerged from nowhere. Many came from merchant families with a traditional interest in the India trade. After 1750, a large proportion of the Company's employees were of Scottish origin. In 1773, a young Scot found that the numbers of his fellow countrymen in Bengal had grown so numerous 'that I shall not be able to enumerate them with the exactness I have hitherto done'. Another source of recruits appears to have been the sons of the Anglican clergy, so establishing a tradition that lasted into much later times. After Plassey and the spread of tales of the great fortunes to be made in Bengal, employment with the East India Company became of interest to widening sections of the British upper classes. A son of Lord Bute, a cousin of the Marquis Cholmondeley, men whose careers were of interest to the King, were among those entering the Company's service after Plassey. Educational standards also rose, and the great public schools, Eton, Harrow, Westminster began their long connection with India.

But there were men of fortune who did not have such backgrounds and behaved in ways the British Establishment considered to be outrageous. The same Richard Smith who had managed to accumulate a large fortune as commander-in-chief in Bengal, and Thomas Rumbold, another nabob, who made one fortune in Bengal and then returned to make another in Madras, fought ostentatiously and expensively for the parliamentary borough of New Shoreham. But, on the whole, the nabobs were reasonably well-bred and neither boorish nor vulgar. This would not, in itself, have prevented British society from considering them inferior, because their fortunes had been made in trade, if nothing more dubious. Perhaps the prejudice that greeted the nabobs in England would have remained on the level of snobbery if they had quietly spent their money on country estates and then lived quietly on them. Some indeed did no more than that, but others sought to use their fortune to obtain political influence and power, and it was against such impertinence that the Establishment rose and girded itself for battle.

3

A Place in the Country
or
the Nabob as Gentleman

[I] *Classical Fronts*

THE country estates which the returning nabobs acquired as soon as possible after their arrival home were an absolute necessity both as sources of political patronage and as symbols of status. Many of the estates purchased already had houses upon them. If they were reasonably modern in style and exhibited the sort of grandeur the purchaser required, all that would be needed was a clean-up and a refurnish. But if they were not, they could be easily demolished and an architect commissioned to design a new one. As most of the nabobs were hoping to identify with the ruling class, the architecture chosen was that of the ruling class. In effect, the nabob put on a Classical or, more precisely a neo-Classical front behind which he could display as much or as little Asian luxury as he chose.

Robert Clive, after doing up the family home at Styche in Shropshire and taking a town house in London's Berkeley Square, decided that he needed a country seat near London, where he could escape the languors of the city and entertain his friends. In the summer of 1769 he acquired the estate of Claremont, near Esher in Surrey, from the widow of that same Duke of Newcastle who had once been his political patron. Remembrance, fond or otherwise, did not prevent him from

34

bargaining the Duchess down from £40,000 to £25,000 for the property.

The existing mansion at Claremont was a substantial building designed by the playwright–architect Sir John Vanbrugh, whose work included Blenheim Palace, home of the Dukes of Marlborough, and Castle Howard in Yorkshire. The park surrounding the house was the work of the great landscape gardener William Kent, who had created an ensemble of lakes, wooded hillocks and rolling grassland adorned with temples, lodges and a belvedere resembling a small castle. Almost at once, Clive decided that he wanted the house pulled down and a new one erected. His reason was simple: Vanbrugh's mansion had been constructed on a low-lying and consequently damp site. Of course, most people could not accept such a practical reason and saw it simply as an act of ostentation: a mansion good enough for a duke could not be good enough for that 'heaven-born general', the victor of Plassey.

The architect chosen by Clive to design the new house was Lancelot 'Capability' Brown, the landscape designer who worked in partnership with Henry Holland. The design they produced, neo-Classical, naturally, had a powerful simplicity, the very opposite of the vulgar ostentation Clive's enemies expected of him. While the old house was being demolished, work on the new began, Clive had the home farm done up as a temporary residence. To accommodate his menagerie of exotic animals; Cape geese, Guinea hens, cyrus birds, as well as spotted deer, the wall of the park was raised in height. Local gossip soon had it that what was ostensibly designed to keep the animals in was actually to keep the Devil out! As for the furnishings of the house, they must be in the latest fashion but there must also be pictures and sculpture and other *objets d'art* for no gentleman's house could be without an art collection. Clive began to collect seriously in 1771, taking advice on what he should buy from the young American artist, Benjamin West, who after settling in London in 1763 became historical painter to King George III and one of the founders of the Royal Academy of Arts. With the help of West and that of a Scottish connoisseur, William Patoun, Clive soon built up the sort of collection that reflected the taste of the times: a *Madonna* by Carlo Dolci, a Guido Reni that was probably a fake, among others. Clive was sneered at, again, by Horace Walpole: 'these learned patrons of taste, the Czarina Catherine the Great, Lord Clive or some Nabob' who were easily gulled into paying large sums for works of dubious quality or authenticity. Nevertheless, with the aid of his two advisers, Clive did acquire a splendid Veronese *Visitation*, a fine Claude, and a Poussin *Finding of Moses*, with which even Walpole could find no fault. All these works were destined for Claremont, for which Clive also planned to commission a set of tapestries from the Gobelins factory of Paris.

In 1773, with the principal aim of buying objects for his art collection, Clive travelled to Italy. In Paris, on the way, he bought furniture as well as pictures and even engaged a sculptor to come and work at Claremont. Once in Rome, Clive bought a number of pictures, a genuine Reni and a Tintoretto *Assumption* among them. But from contemporary Roman painters he would buy nothing. While Clive was in Rome shopping, work continued at Claremont. The outer fabric of the house was almost finished and West was planning the interior and, in particular, the decoration of the Eating Room. The principal features of this room were to be a number of canvases by West himself, depicting the principal events in Clive's Indian career. Only one of these canvases was actually painted, allegedly representing Clive receiving the *diwani* of Bengal from the fugitive Mughal emperor, Shah Alam. This piece of historical tushery displays the event as taking place in a vast pillared hall with all the trappings of eastern monarchy when it actually occurred in Clive's tent with a throne hastily constructed from an armchair covered with a piece of brocade cloth set upon a dining table!

The Eating Room never got past the design stage and though

the decorations would have been whimsical as to fact, they and the elegant Indian ivory furniture with which Clive proposed to furnish it would have made a room eminently suitable for its owner. Unfortunately, Clive never occupied the house, nor bathed in its immense sunken bath of grey marble with piped water laid on, though he may well have availed himself of one of the latest designs in water closets, during a hurried visit.

Following Clive's example, other returned nabobs bought estates and commissioned new country houses within a reasonable coach-ride of London. Sir Thomas Rumbold, who had once been Resident at Patna and a member of the Bengal Council in 1769, returned with a fortune of around £200,000 and commissioned the architect Thomas Leverton to build him a house in the Palladian style at Woodhall Park in Hertfordshire. Following the prescribed pattern, Rumbold became a member of Parliament in 1770 and two years later a Director of the East India Company. With all this, he remained unsatisfied both with the extent of his fortune and with the neo-Classical interiors of his house. He returned to India, though this time to Madras, where he became governor in 1773. But he did not live long enough to enjoy his great house once again. After Rumbold's death, it was acquired by another and almost as disreputable nabob, Paul Benfield, who had made a fortune out of contracts in Madras and loans to the nawab of Arcot.

Warren Hastings's friend and attorney in England, Francis Sykes, had also made a fortune as a Resident, this time at the capital of the fainéant nawab of Bengal at Murshidabad. There Sykes had accepted substantial gifts of jewels from Muhammed Reza Khan, who until dismissed by Hastings, had been the collector of revenue for Bengal. Sykes had also profited in various ways by using the authority of his position to facilitate them, and was rather annoyed when it was suggested that he had defrauded the Company. Sykes did not believe he had, as the profit was there for anyone to take. The choice he faced had, he insisted, been simple: 'whether it should go into a black man's pocket or my own'. He remained convinced that he had made the right choice!

On returning to England, Sykes used some of his profits to become a member of Parliament and later a baronet, and some to build Basildon Park in Berkshire. Designed by John Carr in 1776, the house, built in Bath stone, is described by the architectural historian, Nikolaus Pevsner, as 'the most splendid Georgian mansion of Berkshire'. Not the house of a returned nabob but that of an English country gentleman. Which was exactly what its owner wished to be taken for.

So, too, did Richard Barlow, Warren Hastings's supporter during difficult times in Bengal. Barlow was widely believed to have brought back to England the largest fortune of the 1770s, reckoned at the time to be in the region of £400,000, though this seems to have been rather exaggerated. Barlow had followed paternal example in making a fortune out of India. William Barlow had been governor in Bengal and was dismissed by the Directors of the Company for misconduct in 1749. The extent of that misconduct can be gauged by the fact that on his death twenty years later, his house and estate in Surrey was valued at £10,500, and he had £106,000 in various stocks including those of his erstwhile employers, the East India Company.

Before joining the Bengal Council, Richard Barwell had been Chief at Dacca in what was then east Bengal and had not only taken a cut of the revenue before it reached his employers but also out of the salt trade, a monopoly put up for auction by the Company, and usually bought by employees using Indians as front men. Some of Barwell's profits went on the construction of Stanstead Park in Sussex, another fine neo-Classical mansion.

Barwell's friend, Warren Hastings, spent many years buying back portions of the family estate at Daylesford in Worcestershire which had been sold and the manor house destroyed nearly twenty years before he was born in 1732. Unfortunately, the owner of the principal parts of the estate including the site of the manor house, refused to sell, and it was not until after his death in 1788 that Hastings came into possession of the land. The estate was in decay when Hastings finally acquired it for £11,000. Other parts of the ancestral estate were bought a few acres at a time for inflated prices, but Hastings was determined to restore the estate to its ancestral size and former glory. To do so he needed a suitably grand house. The architect he chose was Samuel Pepys Cockerell, brother of a nabob and brother-in-law of Warren Hastings's private secretary.

In spite of the parlous state of Hastings's finances after the enormous legal costs of his impeachment, no money was spared in the construction of the new house. The finest Cotswold stone was used in its construction, the ironwork came from Birmingham and the fine Wedgwood tiles from Etruria. Workmen and craftsmen were brought down from London and were lodged in the village for a year while they fitted out the house. When the work was finished, the total cost exceeded £54,000. And it still had to be furnished.

By the time of Hastings's acquittal, the house was complete, a dream at last fulfilled. In a valley between gently rising hills and about a mile from the river, Daylesford House stood bright in its fine grey stone. The rooms on the first floor faced south-west with a distant view of a church. There, too, was his library. Among the sculpture were busts of the Prince of Wales, the Duke of York and the owner of Daylesford himself. On the walls, on which perhaps the most spectacular decoration was a set of Persian silver chain-armour, hung a portrait of Hastings on horseback by George Stubbs, some views of India by William Hodges, the painter who had accompanied him on a significant journey to Banaras, and Zoffany's narrative painting of Colonel Mordaunt's Cock Fight at Lucknow with its portraits of the nawab of Oudh and of many others well-known to Hastings. He had for some reason parted with a number of paintings of Indian scenes when he had sold the house in Park Lane and was annoyed that they only raised £125. He wrote to his banker on that occasion to say that few things had 'given me so much vexation as the disgraceful sale of my pictures, I would rather have burnt them'. He was particularly annoyed that a portrait of Shuja-ud-Daulah had gone for 'a mean price' because 'I never intended to part with it, and do not know how it came to be joined to the rest' and asked that it be bought back 'for a sum not much exceeding that at which it was knocked down'.

The furniture at Daylesford was of the most costly materials. Much of it was of ivory, at least in the drawing-room and library. Hastings's collection of Mughal miniatures was distributed around the walls. There was also a separate 'picture-room' which displayed a number of works by old masters, including Rembrandt and Correggio. In this room also hung William Hodges' painting of the terrible storm which had driven Mrs Hastings's boat upon a rock in the Hugli river while she was sailing down to Calcutta to nurse her husband during his first serious illness. The dining-room was sober with the fashionable mahogany furniture of the age. Hastings's bedroom was plain, his wife's rather more extravagant, being decorated in purple and green. At the top of the house were eleven rooms for bachelor visitors and staff. It was a substantial house – it took 167 tons of coal to heat it in 1799 – and it had all the latest modern refinements, including Mr Bramah's water-closet and a muffin stove, and quite a staff of servants.

The gardens were Hastings's particular pride. He delighted in the planning and construction of walks and groves and the sighting of 'prospects'. His landscape gardener's bills frightened his solicitors, but there were Lombardy poplars, almond and lilac, juniper and acacia, tamarisk and tulip trees, magnolias and peaches and mangoes from Bengal. There was a lake, with a bridge, islands and a waterfall.

Apart from the furnishings and paintings, two fireplaces designed by the sculptor, Thomas Banks, drew extensively on Indian motifs. One shows the popular Indian deity of good fortune, the goddess Lakshmi with elephants, and the other a scene of Indian court life including dancers and musicians, and a prince smoking a hookah. The exterior of Daylesford displayed one curious feature which added an Indian touch to an otherwise Classic front. Over the three-storied rotunda forming the entrance of the garden front, Cockerell placed a dome of distinctly Mughal design.

The dome at Daylesford is a sort of tease, a mischievous preview of the house Samuel Pepys Cockerell was later to design for his brother Charles.

[II] *A Taj in the Cotswolds*

In 1794, Colonel John Cockerell purchased the estate of Sezincote in the Gloucestershire Cotswolds. His brother Samuel modernized the existing Jacobean house and gave it a new front. But John died before the renovation of the house was completed and the estate was taken over by his brother, Sir Charles, a friend of Warren Hastings, who had made a reasonable fortune in India. Just when Sir Charles decided that he did not want a Palladian mansion, but an 'Indian' one is not known. Humphrey Repton, another landscape gardener turned architect, told the Prince of Wales in 1805 that he had been consulted by the owner of Sezincote who 'wished to introduce the gardening and architecture which he had seen in India'. Work on the house seems to have started in 1806 or 1807. The design for the house was the responsibility of a sort of committee of four: Sir Charles Cockerell himself, who apparently wanted a version of the Taj Mahal, his brother Samuel, in charge of the actual design, Repton who seems to have been mainly concerned with the layout of the gardens, and Thomas Daniell, as artistic adviser to ensure authenticity.

Daniell was an obvious choice. He and his nephew William had spent nine years in India, many of them in Calcutta, during which they earned a meagre living publishing aquatints of the town. In 1789 they were able to leave Calcutta on a journey up-country. When they reached Rajmahal, the ancient capital of Bihar, they discovered what to them was a new style of building. They immediately set about producing accurate drawings of the Muslim architecture they found around Rajmahal, taking enormous care with their measurements and details. Moving westwards after Rajmahal, they came to other great Muslim buildings around Agra, including the Taj Mahal, and were overwhelmed by their elegant symmetry. Later, the Daniells journeyed south and saw and recorded some of the finest monuments of Hindu architecture.

On their return to England in 1793, the Daniells brought with them some 1,400 drawings. These became the basis of a series of volumes of aquatints, each containing twenty-four prints, published between 1795 and 1808 under the title of *Oriental Scenery*. The effect of these highly picturesque scenes and the careful depiction of exotic buildings on architects and connoisseurs, even on stage-designers, was profound. Sir Charles Cockerell could not have found in Thomas Daniell a more expert expert.

Sezincote itself is a classical villa behind an 'Indian' front with mainly classical interiors. The design is eclectic, a mixture of styles, with 'Hindoo' forms on the ground floor and 'Mogul' above. For the garden, Daniell designed a variety of monuments, including a fountain in the form of a *lingam*, the phallus which is the symbol of the Hindu god Siva, entwined with serpents. There is even a 'Hindoo' bridge, and beneath it a philosopher's chair for meditation on the meaning of the fountain! Originally the domes of the house were painted white to give the impression of marble, and the finials gilded. Together with other features, they helped to make Sezincote a romantic vision of India set in the English countryside.

Sir Charles Cockerell died in 1837, having spent most of his last years abroad. Sezincote itself was attacked by damp and the disapproval of 'modern' architects. Among these was Samuel's son, C.R. Cockerell, who, though he had designed lodges for his uncle in the form of the typical Bengali house from which the bungalow derives, left Sezincote off the list of his father's works published after Samuel's death! Fortunately, Sezincote survives, still a Taj in the Cotswolds, the first – and last – Indian house in Britain, built by a nabob who was so sure of his status that he was not ashamed to advertise his love for the architecture of the country in which he had made his fortune.

4

A Seat in the House

or

The Nabob and Politics

[I] *Ajax and his Shield*

THOSE who most feared the invasion of the nabobs into the privileged club of eighteenth-century politics found a target in the person of Robert Clive, the archetypical nabob, whose reputation, it was suggested, was like 'Ajax's shield in Homer, a Refuge for those who have done great Disservice and have stained the very name and annals of our Country with crimes scarce inferior to the Conquerors of Mexico and Peru'. While still in India and the news of his achievements in Bengal fresh and unsullied by rumours of corruption, Clive had been hailed by William Pitt the Elder, Foreign Secretary for War, as the 'Heaven-born general' who had saved Britain's honour while it was being lost elsewhere, a view enthusiastically endorsed by King George II.

Praise for Clive, however, was by no means universal, and on his arrival in England in July 1760 – a bare three years after Plassey – had, as so often with public heroes, been transferred to others. The most recent of these, James Wolfe, victor at Quebec in 1759, had the advantage of returning home in a coffin rather than, as Horace Walpole put it, 'all over estates and diamonds' as was the case with General Clive. A dead hero must always have the edge on a live one, especially one so demonstrably endowed with the riches of *this* world.

Just how much these riches actually amounted to was the subject of much speculation. The *Annual Register*, a journal which pretended to authority and edited and largely written by Edmund Burke, stated categorically: 'It is supposed the General can realize £1,200,000 in cash, bills and jewels; that his lady has a casket of jewels which are estimated at least at £200,000. So that he may with propriety be said to be the richest subject in the three kingdoms'. As if this was not a sufficiency, there was the income from the famous *jagir* amounting to nearly £30,000 a year.

Though the *Register's* estimate was considerably exaggerated, Clive certainly gave the impression that he was very rich. He made substantial gifts of money to his five sisters and to his parents, as well as an annuity of £500 for his father. Another of the same amount he settled upon his old commander, Stringer Lawrence, and similar sums upon his aunts. He put in hand repairs to Styche Hall, the dilapidated family house at Moreton Say in Shropshire, bought another in the same county at Walcot, and an Irish estate, as well as a London town house in Berkeley Square. Clive had successfully made the nabob's necessary progression from merchant and soldier to country gentleman with a stake in the town. Clive was now thirty-five years of age with a brilliant past behind him and equally brilliant prospects for the future. At the beginning, he does not seem to have been much concerned about building up an 'interest' at India House, the Company's headquarters. He naturally expected to exercise great influence over Indian affairs both political and military. He was in correspondence with his successor in Bengal, and assumed that he would have a say in appointments there. But his real ambition was to make a name and place for himself in English politics, where he believed his 'future power and grandeur' lay.

The first thing he wanted was a peerage, as a reasonable reward for his services. To help in that end, he began to build up an interest in Parliament. Clive himself had tried in 1754 for a seat, but had been defeated. Then he had been supported in his attempt by an opposition peer and the government had rallied enough forces to take the seat. The attempt to enter Parliament had cost Clive a great deal of money, and he was determined that he would not suffer the same fate again. In 1757 he had written to his father, 'if I can get into Parliament I shall be very glad; but no more struggles against the ministry; I choose to be with them'.

Within a few months of Clive's arrival back in England, the old king died and was succeeded by his grandson George III, then aged twenty-one. His accession was followed by a general election in which Clive was elected unopposed for Shrewsbury and his father, Richard, for Montgomery. In addition, a supporter of Clive, John Walsh, won at Worcester, but an attempt to get Clive's cousin George and his brother-in-law Edward Maskelyne in at Penrhyn in Cornwall, despite considerable expenditure, failed. Clive now controlled three votes in Parliament.

The next step was to use his interest in Parliament to acquire a peerage. The new king wanted to introduce his favourite, Lord Bute, into the ministry to which William Pitt, to whom Clive gave his allegiance, was opposed. The Duke of Newcastle, who headed the ministry, was quite prepared to drop Pitt in order to keep in with the new king. All that remained was to entice Pitt's supporters to his side. In the case of Clive, it was clear that the price was a peerage. Newcastle was caught in a dilemma. He had all the dislike of the aristocracy for the 'nabob', the upstart, but he did not want to alienate a wealthy and perhaps useful supporter in Parliament and one who was still something of a hero to the populace. Newcastle compromised by offering Clive an Irish peerage, a sort of second-class honour which did not automatically bring with it a seat in the House of Lords.

Though Clive was disappointed with his Irish peerage, he renamed his Irish estate Plassey after his great victory, so that the name would be enshrined in his title. Clive was convinced that had he been wealthier, he could have bought an English title.

'Believe me,' he wrote to Henry Vansittart, his successor in Bengal, 'there is no other interest in this kingdom but what arises from great possessions, and if after the Battle of Plassey I had stayed in India . . . and acquired the fortune I might have done by this time, I might have been an English Earl with a Blue Ribbon instead of an Irish Peer with the promise of a Red one.' But he was quite wrong. Money alone could not buy a peerage especially in face of the intense class snobbery of eighteenth-century England.

The political scene facing Clive was confused, for British politics were about to enter a period of rapid change. The cause was the new king's desire to revive royal interest in the process of politics. With it began a struggle between the crown and the Whig aristocracy who had for long dominated national affairs. At that time, political parties were not solid, cohesive bodies, but uneasy coalitions of various, and not infrequently antipathetic, groups. Parliament was made up of a number of men whose talents or influence gave them the leadership of such groups. The loyalty of the group to the leader was ensured by a variety of inducements. One such might be the nomination to a 'rotten borough', that is, a borough which up until the reforms of 1832 still returned members to Parliament, even though there were few or no voters left in the constituency. Others were the hope of office for oneself or pensions or lucrative appointments for relatives and friends. Nepotism and corruption were indeed the very commonplace of eighteenth-century politics. Mere brilliance, either of intellect or oratory or even both, were of no use without either influence or a patron. Edmund Burke, who was to wreak his revenge on the nabobs through his impeachment of Warren Hastings, had to attach himself to Lord Rockingham with a generous amount of boot-licking. Even the elder William Pitt, whose speeches and personality allowed him to dominate the House of Commons, would have been ineffective in government without the support of that great Whig, the Duke of Newcastle.

47

Beyond the factions of Whig and Tory were those who had no particular party allegiance and, in general, supported the administration of the day, whatever it was. As long as the Whigs had the favour of the king, this block supported the Whigs. As soon as the new king showed his interest in politics and began treating it as a matter of influence and jobs, this group became his tool. Every combination of factions had to include this group. The consequence was a decade of confusion until the king discovered in Lord North a man who could manipulate both the Commons and the constituencies. North maintained his majority in the lower House through the support of members of this group, men elected by voters who wanted someone to speak for *them* and not for any particular party. Finally, a majority was assured by those members for the rotten boroughs, who made up more than half the membership of the Commons!

These boroughs were in the gift of those who owned them, and one of the best ways of getting into Parliament was to acquire the patronage of one of these local magnates. Another way was to buy a seat simply by buying the property that controlled the votes for it. This was what Clive did, and many of the returning nabobs followed his example, entering Parliament in significant force in the elections of 1768. Criticism soon appeared concerning how they had acquired the money with which to buy these properties. It was not that the politics of the time were less corrupt in Britain than in India, but the means of corruption were of a different order. There existed plenty of opportunities for personal profit in Britain through pensions, or sinecures, or monopolies. But there was very little direct giving of money in contrast with India, where it was the normal practice. This was at least part of the reason for the hostility shown to the nabobs on their arrival in England.

Clive entered the new Parliament as a supporter of Pitt and the Newcastle administration. Among the other members of the Cabinet whom Clive particularly respected was George Grenville, and the two became close friends. When Pitt resigned in

October 1761, Grenville stayed on, and when Newcastle in turn was manoeuvred out of office in the spring of 1762, Grenville remained in the government of the king's friend and Tory, Lord Bute. An attempt was made to gain Clive's support for the new administration. Unfortunately, Clive suspected its intentions towards India. As part of the treaty which ended the Seven Years' War with France, it was suggested that the French possessions in India lost to the British, should be returned. This Clive could not swallow, and voted with the minority against the treaty. He seemed to be proud that he had done so, even though he had, it was said, been offered an English peerage and a sinecure for his cousin, George, to support the administration. 'I still continue,' he wrote to a friend in India, 'to be one of those unfashionable kind of people who think very highly of independency, and to bless my stars, indulgent fortune has enabled me to act according to my conscience.'

A few months later Bute fell from power, and the office of prime minister was filled, in April 1763, by Clive's friend, George Grenville. It seemed as if Clive's time had come, both as a member of Parliament and as adviser on Indian affairs. But nothing came of it. In part this was due to Clive's increasing involvement in the politics of the East India Company. The principal cause of this was his preoccupation with his *jagir* and the threats to its continuance. Clive was obsessed with the matter of the *jagir*. Without the income from it, he would still have been a very rich man and could have concentrated his energies on expanding his political influence on the national level. But he was convinced that 'my future power, my future grandeur, all depend on the receipt of the *jagir* money'. And added, 'I should be a madman to set at defiance those who at present show no inclination to hurt me'.

The Company, by threatening the *jagir* money, would keep Clive in a sort of permanent blackmail, and tied him to the narrowness of the Company's politics, rather than to that of the wider world outside.

Clive wished to influence the policy of the Company towards him and its affairs in India. But he did not want to be Chairman of its Court of Directors. 'I have no thought of ever accepting the Chair; I have neither application, knowledge or time, to understand so laborious an employ. I shall confine myself to the political and military operations . . .' Nevertheless, he sought to control the directors. This was complicated by the fact that the Company was going through a series of changes brought about by Clive's actions in Bengal.

The East India Company was essentially an ordinary commercial undertaking of the times, its existence confirmed by a royal charter periodically renewed. There was nothing *national* about it, being a venture of merchants of the City of London who had been granted a monopoly of the trade to India and the Far East by charter. The Company dealt in spices and cottons, silks, saltpetre, indigo, precious stones, tea from China and other natural products. Its shareholders were represented by a Court of Proprietors meeting once a quarter, or on the demand by nine holders of shares. Every year in March or April the Court fixed the annual dividend and elected a Court of Directors, twenty-four in number. These directors could sit for up to four years but then had to stand down for a year before seeking re-election. The qualification for a vote in the Court of Proprietors was a holding of £500 of stock. However much stock an investor might own, it did not entitle him to more than one vote. The directors had the valuable perquisite of patronage, which naturally was first extended to relations and friends. As the possibilities of acquiring a fortune in India increased, such patronage became a powerful privilege, and consequently much sought after.

The directors were usually merchants of the City with other interests in such things as shipping, distribution, the supply of stores and the like. Very few returned Company servants were made directors. They usually lacked stock or other interest, and on the whole were considered by the City merchants to lack commercial know-how! But events in India converted the

Company from a mere, though wealthy, trading corporation, the 'monied Company' as it was sometimes called, into the *de facto* ruler of large areas of a far-away country with apparently endless potentialities for corporate and private profit. A consequence was a demand for actual Indian experience among the directors. This demand led to the emergence of Lawrence Sulivan and the epic struggle between him and Clive for control of the Company's political machine.

Lawrence Sulivan was an Irishman who had entered the Company's service by the back door. He had gone out to Bombay in the 1740s on his own account, but had been elected to the Bombay Council of the Company by local nomination on account of his proved ability. But Sulivan lacked patronage. His views were also conditioned by the situation of Bombay, a minor outpost of the Company, overshadowed by local powers and its merchants thus disinclined to attempt to interfere in local affairs. Profits were reasonable, but there was no opportunity for acquiring a fortune other than by honest trade. Sulivan, unlike Clive, was not an empire-builder by either nature or conviction. He viewed the extension of the Company's territorial power with apprehension as a threat to the Company's commercial activities and the large scale present-taking that had accompanied it as reprehensible.

In 1753 Sulivan was back in England, determined to take an important role in the Company's affairs. First, he went into the Indian remittance business, then bought a country estate and in 1762 entered Parliament. In 1758 Sulivan was elected Chairman of the Court of Directors. It was a popular appointment, not least with Robert Clive, who wrote to his father from Bengal: 'I cannot conclude this letter without desiring you will make use of all your interest and that of your friends in support of Mr Sulivan and if there should be occasion to lay out any of my money in India Stock in effect my intentions, I desire my attorneys may do so'.

All this changed after Clive's return to England. Very soon

there were hints and rumours going the rounds that the Company might decide to challenge his possession of the *jagir*, and Clive was convinced that Sulivan was behind them. Various other conflicts arose to exacerbate the mutual dislike of the two men. Finally, Clive decided that in order to influence the Company in his favour, he must get rid of Sulivan from the seat of power. Clive marshalled his forces. He had prestige, wealth and the vital support of the returned nabobs who felt they were being discriminated against by the directors and who, the better to coordinate their actions, had formed themselves into the 'Bengal Club'. On his side, Sulivan had the support of the government and the threat to cut off the *jagir* money. Clive and his supporters bought stock and split it into the £500 holdings necessary for a vote in the Court of Proprietors, thus creating several hundred new votes. But for all their wealth, the 'Bengal Club' could not outcall the resources of the City of London especially as it had government backing. Sulivan was returned to power by a substantial majority and was quick to take his revenge: a letter sent to Bengal in April 1763, ordering that all payments of Clive's *jagir* should be stopped. Clive appealed to his friends in Bengal, threatened a law suit against the directors, and tried to get his friend Grenville, not prime minister, to help him. But to no avail.

The victory of Sulivan might have been the end of Clive, but he was saved by the news that reached London in February 1764, of the breach between the British and Mir Kasim, the successor to Mir Jafar as nawab of Bengal, of the massacre that followed at Patna and the military campaign against the nawab, in short that Bengal was 'again became a scene of bloodshed and confusion'. The reaction of the stockholders to this was panicky. The Company's stock fell by fourteen per cent. An attack was mounted against the directors. Sides were taken, with this time the ministry on Clive's side. Then at a meeting of the General Court in March 1764 a 'candid and sensible member', as the *London Magazine* reported, rose and 'as if by inspiration' proposed that Clive should return to Bengal with the combined powers of Governor and Commander-in-Chief. The suggestion was received with cheers and Clive replied, in an obviously prepared speech, that he would do his duty but only if the Court of Directors was as well disposed to him as the Court of Proprietors. In effect, Sulivan would have to go before Clive would go to India. Both sides began to prepare for the annual election of directors.

But first the bargaining – over the *jagir* payments, over Clive's authority over certain appointments in India. Sulivan and his supporters, quick to recognize the threat to their position, assured Clive of their support for his appointment. But Clive refused to work with Sulivan, and in the election a friend of Clive's, Thomas Rous, was appointed to the chair. His majority among the directors was small, but over the next years it increased, so that by the following election Sulivan could only raise seven votes out of the twenty-four directors. The General Court now offered Clive guarantee of the *jagir* money for ten years or life, whichever was the shorter. This he accepted and left England on 4 June 1764. Almost exactly three years later he returned – to almost the same scene of confusion, both in national and Company politics as he had left behind.

In Parliament there did not appear to Clive to be much of a government to give his support to. In 1766 the king had made an attempt to form a national government under Pitt, now Earl of Chatham, as a leader above party. Unfortunately, Chatham's health broke down early in the following year, which left the administration, and the country, leaderless until the reins of power were rather feebly grasped by the Duke of Grafton. In the absence of strong leadership, the House of Commons was a loose collection of factions. The elections of 1768 which took place just before Clive's return, brought a large number of nabobs into the House. Clive's group consisted of his relatives and John Walsh, his agent, and his one-time secretary, Henry Strachey. Francis Sykes, who had been resident at Murshidabad and retired from India with a substantial fortune; General John Carnac, a confidant of Clive; Lord Pigot, who had seen distinguished service in Madras, and his two brothers; and Robert Palk, another ex-governor of Madras, were not of Clive's group but were not hostile. Indeed, like Clive, they all had fortunes acquired in India to defend. There were others who were hostile to Clive. John Johnstone, who had clashed with Clive during the latter's second term in Bengal, and Sir Robert Fletcher, cashiered by Clive for involvement in the so-called White Mutiny in the Company's army in 1766, were decidedly unfriendly. So was Sir Hector Monro, the victor of Buxar, who thought that Clive had discriminated against him in favour of his friend Carnac, and Sir Eyre Coote, who had been a military critic of Clive ever since Plassey.

The Company's relations with Parliament and the government were as complicated as ever. Government interference in the Company's affairs had been stimulated by the news, in the spring of 1766, of Clive's acceptance from the fugitive Mughal emperor Shah Alam, of the legal right of rule in Bengal. The result had been speculation in Company stock and demands for an increase in the dividend. Chatham, then in power, had responded to this with an attempt at forcing the Company to give up a share in the Bengal revenues to the government. Chatham was also convinced that Bengal was too big for the Company to handle on its own.

The attack on the Company was opened by Alderman William Beckford (father of the future author of *Vathek*). According to Luke Scrafton, Beckford 'took an opportunity to abuse the Company as an unconstitutional monopoly, and that their conduct merited the enquiry of Parliament; that they had a revenue of two millions in India, acquired God knows how, by unjust wars with the natives. That their servants came home with immense fortunes obtained by rapine and oppression, yet the Proprietors received no increase in dividend: that it was necessary to know how these revenues were consumed and whence these oppressions so loudly talked of, and therefore he should next day move the House that the affairs of the East India Company should be laid before Parliament'.

The attempt to bully the Company had a simple cause: the desire to extract money for the State from a rich corporation dependent on the State for its privileges and one, furthermore, vulnerable because of widespread jealousy of those privileges. The attempt to impose a solution failed because of Chatham's own decline and fall. But the State did not abandon its claims and negotiations were opened. In 1767 an agreement was reached by which the Company would pay the State £400,000 a year for two years, and the government in turn imposed a limit on the dividend of ten per cent for one year.

Another round of negotiations took place in 1769. Clive disapproved of a new settlement by which the Company's annual payment was extended for five years in return for allowing the dividend to rise to twelve-and-a-half per cent. But Clive and his group did not challenge it in Parliament because feelings against the nabobs were rising and no one wished to draw attention to themselves.

The Company's internal affairs were also confused. Clive's supporter Thomas Rous still held the Chair, but the opposition was stirring once again. Returning nabobs were spending money on the purchase of stock, splitting it and forming groups, most of them against Clive. Among them were Robert Fletcher and John Johnstone's brother William. Sulivan, too, was beginning to raise his head above the parapet. George Grenville gave Clive some very good advice: 'Keep yourself in the honourable state of a public man, only attributing your advice and assistance when asked to preserve to this country that great empire which you had so great a share in acquiring'. Unfortunately, Clive did not take it. He was still in fear that his *jagir* money might be stopped.

Clive had reason to be apprehensive. There was very little doubt that a campaign was being set in motion to discredit Clive and the nabobs who huddled behind his shield. The first sign was the return to power of Lawrence Sulivan in April 1769. Within a month of his election, bad news from India induced a catastrophic fall in the value of East India stock. Many people were ruined or nearly ruined, including Edmund Burke and Sulivan himself. One of the consequences was the despatch of Warren Hastings to India. Another was the growth of criticism over the general competence of the Company to run its own affairs.

As if this were not bad enough, a terrible famine struck the Company's territories in Bengal in 1769–70, in which between a third and a half of the rural population perished. Ugly rumours of food hoarding and profiteering by the Company's servants began to be heard. Horace Walpole, whose ear was often at the right keyhole, remarked that 'the oppressions of India and even of the British settled there under the rapine and cruelties of the servants of the Company had now reached England and created great clamour here. Some books had been published . . . which carried the accusations home to Lord Clive; and . . . represented him as a monster in assassination, usurpation and extortion, with heavy accusation of him monopolizing in open defiance of the orders of the Company . . . To such monopolies were imputed the late famine in Bengal and the loss of three millions of the inhabitants. A tithe of these crimes was sufficient to inspire horror'.

The horror felt was disseminated by the periodicals that formed public opinion, and the publicity came, as one nabob put it, at 'an unlucky time, mankind in general being willing to suspect that so many great fortunes cannot be fairly acquired'. Indeed the full impact of the returning nabobs was just beginning to take effect. The image of the nabob, ostentatious, vulgar and ill-bred, was being propagated, though apart from one or two they were usually men of good manners and good education. It suited the caricaturists and pamphleteers to transfer the sins of the few to the relatively innocent many. And, of course, even the 'innocent' were rich.

Pamphlet followed pamphlet and book followed book, most of them hostile to Clive and all widely read. The press was full of scurrilous attacks. An open letter to Clive in the *Public Advertiser* began: 'If the opium has not blunted every nerve, if you have one latent spark of feeling left in your whole frame, I will search out the place where it inhabits and plant a dagger there . . .' These attacks were generally shrugged off by Clive. But a new and far more potentially wounding assault was about to take place, and in the House of Commons.

The proximate cause was the collapse of the Company's credit. For some time the Company had relied on the revenues from Bengal to pay for the annual 'investment'. Normally, the sale of goods sent home provided the cash to meet the Company's liabilities at home. But the surplus of revenue in Bengal declined substantially because of the famine and defects in the local administration. There was also a heavy demand on the Company's cash available in London to redeem bills of exchange used by its own employees as a means of transmitting their fortunes back to England. The Company found itself suffering from what are now called 'cash-flow' problems. The Bank of England refused to renew its loan to the Company, and the government would not give up its annual £400,000. The threat of government intervention was now so strong that the Company, in an effort to stave it off, presented a bill to Parliament for the reform of its administration in Bengal.

The Judicature Bill which the Company proposed involved a new Charter of Justice for Bengal, the barring of the governor and members of council from trade and various provisions for strengthening the Company's control over its servants. This last Clive took as an attack upon himself, and launched into a response that was described by Chatham, a great orator himself, as 'one of the most finished pieces of eloquence he had ever heard in the House of Commons'.

Clive began his speech by saying that when he arrived in Bengal in 1765, there had been three paths open to him. 'One was strewed with abundance of fair advantages. I might have put myself at the head of the government as I found it.' But that would have meant condoning abuses. He could have left Bengal to its fate, but that would have been the path of 'folly and cowardice'. The 'third path was intricate. Danger and difficulties were on every side. But I resolved to pursue it. In short, I was determined to do my duty to the public although I should incur the odium of the whole settlement [i.e. the British in Bengal]. The welfare of the Company required vigorous exertion, and I took the resolution of cleansing the Augean stables. It was that conduct', he continued, 'which has occasioned the public papers to teem with scurrility and abuse against me, ever since my return to England. It was that conduct which occasioned these charges. But it was that conduct which enables me now, when the day of judgment is come, to look at my judges in the face'.

Clive continued to defend himself over the question of monopolies and their effects. He 'could not understand,' he said, 'how a monopoly of salt, betel nut and tobacco in the years 1765 and 1766 could occasion a want of rain and scarcity of rice in the year 1770 . . . I know no more about it than the Pope of Rome'.

After protesting that he had spoken for too long, and receiving loud shouts of 'Go on, go on!' Clive waxed lyrical on the temptations facing a young man newly arrived in Calcutta. The newcomer observes that former employees like himself after a year there 'live in splendid apartments or have houses of their own, ride upon prancing Arabian horses and in palanquins and chaises; they keep seraglios, make entertainments and treat with champagne and claret'. When he speaks to his Indian clerk about it, the reply is that he too could live that way as long as he gives him the authority to act in his name. 'Hence, sir, arises the clamour against the English gentleman in India', not because of his own acts but of those of his clerk who 'commits acts of violence in his name'.

Clive then turned from the lyrical to the abrasive, attacking almost everybody indiscriminately; the General Court, the

Company as a whole, for treating the revenues of Bengal as 'rather a South Sea Bubble than as anything solid and substantial', the Directors, and the government of Bengal. This was a great mistake on Clive's part. To attack everybody meant to antagonize everybody or at least most of those who might perhaps have remained neutral. Clive's defence had been masterly and should have been left to its own virtues. All he had done with his criticism of others was to give a new lease of life to criticism of himself.

The debate that followed brought charge and countercharge, until Colonel John Burgoyne (later to achieve some notoriety as the loser of the Battle of Saratoga in the American War of Independence), a private member who supported the government, proposed that before the Judicature Bill be voted upon the House should set up a Select Committee 'to inquire into the nature, state and condition of the East India Company, and the British affairs in the East Indies'. This had an almost universal appeal to the members of the House and was accepted without a division. The setting up of the Select Committee was a direct consequence of the barrage of vague charges put up by Clive, and he was to suffer somewhat at its hands. He might have suffered worse had not the majority on the Committee been reasonably open-minded. But there were also a number of his enemies determined that he would not get away unscathed.

The Select Committee looked into everything back to the times of Siraj-ud-daulah and Plassey. Clive was closely questioned, particularly over the matter of presents from Mir Jafar after he had been placed upon the throne. Clive defended himself with an exaggeration of the temptation put in his way and of the modesty of his reaction. 'A great prince,' he thundered, 'was dependent on my pleasure, an opulent city lay at my mercy; its richest bankers bid against each other for my smiles; I walked through vaults which were thrown open to me alone, piled on either hand with gold and jewels! Mr Chairman, at this moment I stand astonished at my own moderation!'

The first report of the Committee, awash with stories of presents and intrigues, was submitted to Parliament on 24 May 1772. Clive came out of it comparatively unscathed. The Company, however, did not. Clive, in fact, seemed to profit from all the hullabaloo. The king was friendly, even Lord North seemed generally favourable. In June, Clive was installed as a Knight of the Bath, and in October as Lord Lieutenant of the County of Shropshire. Was an English peerage far behind? As for the Company, its financial state was going from worse to worse. The government, with some reluctance, began to consider a Regulating Bill of its own.

As the debate continued, it became clear to Clive and the other nabobs that the directors of the Company were determined to make them scapegoats for the Company's ills. All sorts of revelations regaled members of the House. On one occasion, an irregular tax called the 'Matoot' (*Mahatut*) was being discussed when Francis Sykes, who had benefited from it, foolishly asked an old clerk from the East India House, who was testifying, what exactly the tax was used for. The man replied: 'Mr Sykes received annually 24,000 rupees for his table, 18,000 for his dress and for his *munshi* (interpreter) 18,000 more'. Sykes sat down, red in the face, with members staring at him. The press were quick to dub him 'Squire Matoot', another term of abuse for the nabobs.

The attacks on Clive in the periodicals and newspapers continued unabated, and *Lloyd's Evening Post* took up the use of the Sykes' nickname in announcing the runners in the 'great Matoot Sweepstakes' for ten thousand lacks (10 billion rupees), one of the entrants being a 'bay horse Jagir, got by Nabob out of Rapino's dam, full sister of Satan'.

In May 1773 Clive was compelled to defend himself once again in the House of Commons. On one occasion he spoke for nearly two-and-a-half hours. Horace Walpole wrote that Clive's speech 'was not a piece of regular and set oratory, but the artful effusions of a man, master of his cause, of himself, and of the passions of others which he raised, interested or amused, as he found necessary . . . while ministers and the Parliament sunk before him, he shone eminently as a real great man, who had done great things, and who had the merit of not having committed more (perhaps not worse) villainies'.

Clive claimed that he had been interrogated by the members of the Select Committee as if he had been caught stealing sheep. He savaged Sulivan, who was in the House, for being 'so assiduous in my affairs that really, Sir, it appears he has entirely neglected his own'. His speech was punctuated with applause and laughter, particularly when he drew a picture of the directors 'devouring the turtle soup and all kinds of viands out of season, and swilling themselves with whole hogsheads of claret, champagne and burgundy' at the expense of the stockholders of the Company. As for the Regulating Bill, which the debate was supposed to be about, he drew a picture of government patronage which would lead to some 'noble Duke, or other high in blood, high in female connections, appointed Viceroy or Governor-General'. As for those 'first rate geniuses who spent their thousands' in gambling houses, they would be made members of Council in India and 'instead of returning home Nabobs, as we have done, they will all return Great Moguls'.

Again Clive had produced a speech that entertained rather than convinced. His enemies remained vocal and were quick to point out their disapproval of Clive's tone. *The Public Advertiser* published a warning: 'Perhaps a certain Assembly may pluck up a resolution which may rescue them from that *contempt* with which you seem to treat them. Then, my Lord beware of PAINS AND PENALTIES!'

The answer of Clive's enemies in the House was to encourage Burgoyne to present his Committee's reports for debate. This he did, in the most provocative manner. 'We have in India,' he declared, 'revolution upon revolution, extortion upon extortion. In the whole history of mankind, I defy mankind to produce such a continued system of oppression.' The debate that followed was stormy. The government did not make clear its collective view, maintaining that ministers spoke only in their personal capacity. Without a ministerial lead the result was highly confusing, resulting, however, in an exciting finish with Burgoyne proposing three very general resolutions to the House, which were adopted.

1 That all territorial acquisitions made by subjects belonged to the Crown.
2 That it was illegal for private persons to appropriate the revenues of such possessions.
3 That there had been appropriation of such revenues.

The first of these was a direct challenge to the Company, the second and third were designed to point the finger at Clive and his associates.

Clive recognized the danger contained in the proposals, and so did the public press. The *Morning Advertiser* announced that 'On Friday next, the public censure of the Commons of Great Britain will be followed, it is expected by a vote for RESTITUTION'. But in spite of appearances, perhaps all was not lost. Edward Gibbon believed that though 'the hounds go out again next Friday . . . the more sagacious ones have no idea they shall kill'. Friday came and went with the debate postponed, but only until the following Wednesday. Then Burgoyne informed the House that he intended to put forward a resolution that Clive had 'illegally acquired the sum of £234,000 to the dishonour and detriment of the State'. This time Clive's defence lacked drama but not pathos. 'Do I stand condemned by an *ex post facto* resolution for receiving presents sixteen years ago? . . . I can never believe that this House will ever adopt such a horrid idea, such a shocking, dreadful, detestable idea as to punish a man for what he could not know he could be guilty of . . . I am not afraid to meet adversity . . . I may be broken but I will never stoop to ill-fortune, I may be distressed, I may be ruined, but as long as I have a conscience to defend me, I will always be happy . . . I have only one thing more, that is a humble request to the House. I make it not for myself, but for them, the request is this, when they come to decide upon my honour, they will not forget their own.'

With this plea, Clive, in tears, left the House. A witness, that same Francis Sykes who had suffered by foolishly opening his mouth at the wrong time, and would certainly suffer more if the vote went against Clive, wrote: 'I never suffered more in my own mind when I was a prisoner of Siraj-ud-daula than I did that very night,' and he added, 'you may easily judge at Lord Clive's situation when he did not know that he had sixpence to call his own in the morning'. The House itself was not unmoved by Clive's speech, indeed there seemed to be a sense of embarrassment among the members. Even the newspapers thought that Clive was being hounded and one journal compared his situation to that of Admiral Byng, some seventeen years before, who had been shot, in Voltaire's immortal words, *'pour encourager les autres'*.

Clive had to wait for two days before he would learn his fate. Burgoyne again opened the proceedings by proposing a motion very much the same as the one he had put before. The House was split, so was the government. The solicitor-general, Alexander Wedderburn, led Clive's defence while his colleague, Lord Thurlow, the attorney-general, was against. The prime minister, Lord North, and other members of the government did not speak against Clive, but when it came to the vote, came down against him. But the feeling grew that Clive had achieved things of value to the State which outweighed criticism of any particular action. Burgoyne's motion was slowly whittled away until Wedderburn moved: 'That Robert, Lord Clive, did, at the same time, render great and meritorious services to his country'. The motion was passed without a division. Clive had been vindicated.

'Lord Clive,' wrote Edmund Burke, shortly after the debate, 'has thus come out of the fiery trial much brighter than he went into it. His gains are now recorded and not only not condemned but actually approved by Parliament. His reputation, too, for ability stands higher than ever'. But Clive was not immune to criticism outside the House. It was soon suggested that bribery had been involved. Horace Walpole, forever acid-tongued, suggested that Clive had corrupted a 'secret junto' at Court and that the king had something to do with the verdict. This was quite untrue, even though some of the so-called 'King's Friends' had voted for Clive. In fact the king, though rather relieved at the result, was 'amazed that private interest could make so many forget what they owe to their country, and come to a resolution that seems to approve of Lord Clive's rapine. No one thinks his services greater than I do, but that can never be reason to commend him in what certainly opened the door to the fortunes we see daily made in that country [India]'.

Clive and the rest of the nabobs were off the hook, Ajax's shield had certainly given them protection, though it would not do so for much longer. In two years, Clive would be dead. The East India Company's situation, however, was perilous. It had asked the government for a loan of £1 million. In return, it got an Act 'for establishing certain regulations for the better manage-ment of the East India Company, as well in India as in Europe'. By the terms of the new Act, the Company got its loan but had its dividend fixed at 6 per cent, surplus profits would go to the State. It was given a new charter but only for six years. The stock qualification for voting was doubled, and a quarter of the directors would have to retire each year.

As for affairs in India, the act provided for a governor-general in Bengal with the authority to 'superintend' the Company's settlements at Madras and Bombay. The governor-general was to have a salary of £25,000 a year and he was to have four councillors each paid the substantial sum of £10,000 a year to assist him. In the Council the governor-general would not be supreme; he was only given a casting vote. Not only that, but there was to be a watchdog. A Supreme Court with authority over all British subjects was to be set up in Calcutta with the

Mir Jafar with Clive, 1773

Sir Charles Cockerell

Sir Thomas Rumbold

Richard Barwell and his son by Barlow,
after Sir Joshua Reynolds

Sir Philip Francis, by Lonsdale

Sezincote, the South Front

Claremont, the Seat of Robert Clive

Woodhall Park, Herts

Basildon House, Berkshire, the Seat of Sir Francis Sykes

Siraj-ud-Daula with Alivardi Khan, Murshidabad

European Officer & dog, Murshidabad

Charles Cockerell and his wife, 1789.
Painting by Francesco Renaldi

The Ghost of Omichund.
Cartoon from the Westminster Magazine

A New Scene for the
Proprietors of India Stock.
Cartoon featuring Clive

responsibility of approving the legislative acts of the Council. All despatches previously sent only to the directors were now to go also to a government minister. Having caught the high officials of the Company, the Act then lashed out at all its employees. There would in future be no private inland trading and the taking of 'presents' was expressly forbidden. One proposal at least was eliminated as part of a deal between the government and its supporters among the nabobs. This was a clause prohibiting trade relations between the Company's servants and foreign merchants in India. Charles Jenkinson, who prepared the clause, remembered that 'it was withdrawn at the request of several servants of the Company who had raised fortunes in India, and who were exceedingly alarmed at it and promised their support to the other provisions of the Bill if this was omitted'.

There was a certain amount of lobbying for the new post of governor-general. Warren Hastings seems to have gathered support very quickly, possibly because of Sulivan who still controlled valuable votes in Parliament. The only person of consequence whose views were neither canvassed nor considered was Hastings himself. Instead, he had the eulogy of Lord North who proposed him as 'a person who, though flesh and blood, had resisted the greatest temptations, though filling great offices in Bengal during the various revolutions that had been felt in that country, never received a single rupee at any one of them, and whose abilities and intense application would be apparent to any gentleman who would consider what he had done during the first six months of his administration!' It was one of the very few occasions in eighteenth-century English politics when the absence of parliamentary connections, wealth or family influence, was actually an advantage.

The new Act was a mass of inconsistencies. Ostensibly it was an attempt to bring together the old system of the Company with a new system imposed by the government. There was, however, no doubt that the new regime Lord North envisaged in India was both inquisitorial and reforming. One of the new councillors 'conceived that we are to be armed with extraordinary powers to correct enormous abuses'. The government supported Warren Hastings as the new governor-general, but disapproved of his supporters in the Company, and therefore, by implication, of his acts as Governor of Bengal before the passing of the Act! It was but a short step from this for the new councillors to declare that they were 'the representatives of the government deputed to act generally for the nation; in contradistinction to Mr Hastings ... who may be supposed to act for the Company!'

It was a recipe for conflict. As for Hastings, Lawrence Sulivan wrote to the new governor-general: 'It will require all your philosophy to bear with temper the Parliamentary system which in great degree annihilates the Company's powers and privileges, disgraces and degrades the service in India and essentially wounds your own authority ... As the minister and the new Council publicly profess an implicit dependence on Mr Hastings, I am still willing to hope that those excellent rules you have and mean to establish for the perfect government of Bengal will be confirmed and pursued ... Yet even with harmony in your Council (so much to be desired) your task is extremely arduous – Scripture says it is impossible to serve two masters.'

[II] *Serving Two Masters*

At noon on 19 October 1774, the siesta of most of Calcutta's inhabitants was disturbed by the roar of guns from Fort William. But the governor and the leading British were very much awake at that hottest hour on a hot and sultry day, for the sound of the guns heralded the arrival of the three new councillors and the judges of the new Supreme Court authorized by Lord North's Regulating Act. The fourth of the new councillors, Richard Barwell, was with the governor at his house. So too were the members of the old Council, except for the senior member who

66

had gone down to the landing-place to greet the new arrivals.

The reception had not been auspicious. One of the new councillors was angered by the fact that the salute of guns numbered only seventeen when he believed that it should have been twenty-one. The garrison of the fort had not been called out and there had not even been a guard of honour. His first despatch home was full of complaint. At Government House, too, there had been no ceremony; as one of the councillor's party put it, 'Mr Hastings might have put on a ruffled shirt'. Even a banquet at two o'clock could not reduce the councillors' suspicion that it was Hastings's intention 'to lower us in the eyes of the natives'. The battle lines were instantly established. The three men from London – the majority in the new council – against the governor-general. Hastings was to suffer badly from the effects of Lord North's Act for, as one of the Company's friends in Parliament had said, 'it was a medly of inconsistencies, dictated by tyranny, yet bearing throughout each line the mark of ignorance'. In the hands of the three new councillors the Act became a tool of personal hatreds and private ambitions.

Lord North's aim in the appointment of councillors had been to please both the king and Parliament. George III was very much concerned with extending his personal authority and was not unwilling to acquire the patronage which control of the Company would bring. The king also disliked the Company. Two of the councillors were king's men: General John Clavering and Colonel George Monson. Clavering, at fifty-one, had seen some undistinguished action and held a diplomatic post at one of the German principalities. His political connections were with the king's supporters and against democracy and radicalism. He was believed to be honest and known to be bad-tempered. He was also obsessed with detail, particularly that of protocol. The king assumed that as senior in Council he would succeed Hastings as governor-general. To reinforce his authority, Clavering was also appointed commander-in-chief. This made Clavering all the more irritated when he learned that the Chief

Justice of the new Supreme Court would have precedence over him, and immediately after the governor-general.

Colonel Monson was very much the same type as Clavering. A brave soldier, now fifty-three, he was politically naive. Though he had Indian experience, it had been confined to the south and he knew nothing about Bengal, Monson had been a member of Parliament and was supposed to have the patronage of Clive.

The king was very satisfied with the nomination of Clavering and Monson. Their lack of experience did not matter much; it was their loyalty that counted. But there was no point in having patronage if there was no profit from it. The Company had to remain a viable trading entity and that could hardly be left to soldiers, even loyal ones. Hastings had been picked as governor-general partly because he was an essentially neutral, non-partisan figure in political terms and highly experienced in commercial as well as diplomatic matters. It would be sensible, the king believed, that there should be another member of Council with Bengal experience and preferably one who 'acted in conjunction with Mr Hastings'. Lord North had agreed; 'if any accident should happen to Mr Hastings', there should be 'some person in the Council already acquainted with the country'. It was also wise 'not to discourage the Gentlemen at present there in Bengal, by totally excluding them from the Council. The councillor whose abilities are spoken as considerable is one Richard Barwell'. It was an odd choice, but Hastings was to be grateful for it. It was said that Clive had advised North to appoint Barwell.

Barwell had been born in Calcutta where his father had at one time been governor. Barwell had a simple ambition – he intended to leave India a very rich man and he had no intention of staying long in the country to do it. He wanted to enjoy his wealth in England and while he was still young enough to get the most pleasure from it. He was involved in all manner of private trading including sectors specifically banned to members of Council. He supervised the affairs of a number of the more notorious 'nabobs', and with the aid of his father, who was frequently a director of the Company, he was able to influence matters in London. His private life was wrapped in all the luxuries money could buy. He gambled heavily, he over-ate (like so many of his contemporaries), and his mistress was an English woman, Mrs Thompson.

For the first year, Barwell was in almost continuous conflict with Hastings. He criticized the governor's actions in well-argued minutes and complained to the directors in London. His main objection was that the new governor wanted to do everything himself and reduce the members of Council to mere cyphers. The conflict between them, Barwell insisted, was not of his making but entirely due to Hastings who could not 'yield to another the least share of reputation that might be derived in the conduct of his government'. The coming together of the two men, Barwell fat but mentally nimble and a shrewd judge of character, and Hastings, small and thin and quick to recognize talent when he saw it, was slow. Barwell from dislike came to recognize Hastings' 'very extensive abilities', and Hastings from irritation at Barwell's 'talents for opposition', came to the opinion that he had 'solid judgement, much greater fertility of official resources than I have'.

With the balance nicely held between the two men from Bengal and the two agents of the king, the fifth appointment was a matter for great care and consideration. He must side with Clavering and Monson on matters of consequence and so produce a majority in the Council. A number of names were canvassed but the choice fell on Philip Francis. It was not a name that conjured up a picture of power or influence, personal or family. Francis was thirty-three, born in Dublin but educated in London. His father had been chaplain to the family of Henry Fox, first Lord Holland, father of Charles James Fox, and it was through the father's influence in that quarter that a door was opened for Francis. It had led to an appointment as a clerk in the office of the Secretary of State, a diplomatic mission to Portugal and the position of first clerk at the War Office. There Francis began a close friendship with Christopher D'Oyley, a supporter of Clive.

In politics Francis had not been conspicuously successful. He had taken as his patron John Calcraft, who had been Henry Fox's deputy as Paymaster but had deserted him for Chatham. When Calcraft died in 1772 he left a legacy to Francis and the promise of a seat in Parliament. Both were welcome as Francis had resigned from the War Office earlier in the year with his friend D'Oyley. He had been looking about for a job and had even been contemplating going to America or even to Asia – in effect, anywhere he might find some profit. Who put his name forward is not known.

It was said later, and by members of his family, that the appointment was a bribe, not to buy a councillor but to buy silence. At the end of January 1769 there had begun to appear in the *Public Advertiser* a series of letters signed 'Junius'. They were eloquent and often vicious attacks on the king and the government, first of the Duke of Grafton and then of Lord North. There had been seventy letters in all until they ceased in January 1772, the most notorious being the thirty-fifth, which warned the king that as he had acquired his crown 'by one revolution' it could be 'lost by another'. The authorship of the letters was unknown – and still is not satisfactorily established – but Francis could have written them, and the appointment to Bengal, a way of seeing that he wrote no more. At all events, no more were written.

As soon as he heard of his appointment, Francis visited Robert Clive at his house in Shropshire, and it was there that he first met Clavering. He laid down his lines with Clive's friends and of course with the government. He advised North that the Council must have full powers, and, guarding his future, he obtained a promise that the seat in Parliament he had been promised would be kept open for him at the next election. But governments came and went, so as extra insurance he opened up communications with Edmund Burke. Henry Strachey, Clive's former secretary, advised him to send information to Burke from India 'so that he may remember you in any opportune compliment in the House of Commons'.

There is little doubt that Francis thought he would make a better governor-general than Hastings, certainly better than Clavering who seemed likely to succeed when the time came to get rid of Hastings. Francis was not a man without qualities. He was very much a product of the 'age of enlightenment'. He was intelligent, widely-read. He was not a Christian and hated priests. He studied the new science of economics and maintained that he was a man of principles. He enjoyed a drinking bout and pornography. His home life was pleasant, though he was a stern husband and father. His wife, Elizabeth Mackrabie, was left behind to bring up their six children. Francis fully intended that in a Council divided between Hastings and Barwell, and Clavering, Monson and himself, he would control the majority. Clavering and Monson were nonentities. So too was Barwell, and he might be bought. The fight was to be between Francis and Hastings – and it was to be a fight to the death.

Francis had allies on various levels, though their alliance was conditional. They were against Hastings, but not necessarily for Francis. Some of the British in Bengal who disliked Hastings for his lack of corruption and his insistence upon the reality rather than the appearance of reform, had powerful friends at home. The most important of these was Joseph Fowke. His principal connections were with the Clive faction, his brother-in-law was Clive's principal agent in England, and his nephews represented Clive's financial interests in Madras.

In the, as yet, loose conspiracy of self-interest were members of the new Supreme Court. Hastings had a friend – and a very old one – in the chief justice. Elijah Impey had been at Westminster School with the governor-general and they had remained close. Impey had influence with the government, especially through Lord North's attorney-general, Thurlow. But Impey had his enemies among the other justices. Stephen Lemaistre and John Hyde were arrogant men of little distinction and therefore all the more conscious of their rights and privileges. Sir Robert Chambers, on the other hand, who had almost been appointed chief justice, had been professor of law at Oxford and a friend of Dr Johnson, and had carried a letter from Johnson to Hastings which included the sentence: 'That he is going to live where you govern, may justly alleviate the regret of parting'. But Chambers had the promise of Lord North that he would be given a seat on the Council. He was, if not a king's man, a North man, and, as he later claimed, he never opposed 'those gentlemen in whom the government of those provinces was meant to be lodged'.

The hostility of the new councillors was quickly revealed. The day after their arrival they met together in Council with Hastings and Barwell and spent much time wrangling over the way in which their arrival and the new system of government should be announced to the ignorant people of Bengal. Clavering insisted on an impressive military display. They adjourned, at Hastings's request, for five days. It is possible that Hastings considered resignation. The hostility of the new councillors was blatantly obvious. He was in a minority, perhaps a minority of one. But he had received a number of letters from England advising him to stay on and indicating that he was not without influential friends at home, and he probably did not take long to decide to stay. Apart from his own feeling of resentment and even of aggression, there was the underlying motive of self-preservation. He had not made enough to retire.

Hastings's decision to carry on and fight won him the support of Barwell who declared himself openly on Hastings's side: 'I am with the governor-general, whose ideas are certainly right, whatever light they may be represented in, and whatever might be thought of them in Europe'. When the Council met again Hastings needed a friend. He hoped to divert his enemies – he recognized them now as such – with a long statement on revenue matters, as well as one on the relations with Indian states. The new councillors found revenue not only boring but incomprehensible. They could hardly make much of a case against Hastings out of something that not only they but those they wished to influence could not understand. But the survey of 'foreign affairs' included the Rohilla campaign.

The view from Calcutta when Hastings had assumed office in 1772 was hardly reassuring. The Mughal emperor, Shah Alam, who had remained a pensioner of the British at Allahabad after Clive's treaty with him, had taken himself back to Delhi in 1771. The British had not approved of the decision and had neither hindered nor helped his return. But they virtually stopped payment of the subsidy guaranteed under the treaty. The Marathas had concluded a treaty with Shah Alam and had escorted the emperor back to Delhi in return for a promise of subsidy and other material advantages. Unfortunately, Shah Alam was penniless. All that he possessed of any value were the provinces of Allahabad and Kora which had been assigned to him by Clive. Why not suggest that the Marathas go and capture the two provinces? Perhaps they might get involved with the British and be defeated.

The Marathas were already planning an attack on Rohilkhand, an area between the possessions of the nawab of Oudh and those of Delhi. Its inhabitants were mainly Hindus but they were ruled by a minority of some 50,000 Rohillas, tough Muslim Afghans, famous as mercenary soldiers. The invader Ahmad Shah Abdali had left a Rohilla behind in Delhi when his men forced him to return home. That man's son was still a power in the imperial capital. The present leader of the Rohillas was Hafiz Khan, whom Burke and his friends confused with the Persian poet and, from the confusion, made of these rough and semi-literate tribesmen paragons of the arts and 'the most honourable nation in the world'.

The first problem posed for Hastings by Maratha intentions was that of the security of Oudh. That state formed a buffer between Bengal and the anarchy of Delhi and beyond. If it fell to the Marathas or any other combination it would bring a hostile power right to the borders of the Company's dominions. That could not be allowed to happen. British relations with the ruler of Oudh, the nawab Shuja-ud-daulah, were regulated by the treaty concluded with him after the battle of Buxar in 1764. His security and that of the British were mutually dependent, but he was disliked by most of the British military establishment though they had no objection to milking him for 'extra expenses' when he called upon the Company's army for assistance against external aggression from the Marathas, say, or even – anything was possible in the India of the time – the Marathas in combination with the Rohillas? The British were obliged by treaty to aid Shuja, but Hastings was not anxious to get involved.

Unfortunately, the commander-in-chief, Sir Robert Barker, persisted in interfering in matters which were not his immediate concern. When a request for at least the promise of assistance came from Shuja, a force commanded by Barker was sent into Oudh, but he was ordered not to act unless forced to do so. Barker took on himself the role of mediator and concluded an agreement with Shuja and the Rohillas to go to their assistance against the Marathas. In return the Rohillas were to pay Shuja the sum of 4 million rupees. Hastings condemned Barker's action as endangering the whole careful system he was hoping to build, saying it would probably lead the British into 'an unnecessary breach with the Marathas'.

But no alliance was stable in India. Shuja began to fear that the Rohillas would make an accommodation with the Marathas and help them in their projected attack on Allahabad and Kora. They were more likely to do so if the British vacillated about their aid. When in January 1773 the Marathas entered Rohilkhand, they found all the allies waiting for them. The Marathas were not really ready to fight the British. They were by no means at their full strength, but their leaders had hoped that the general dread of Maratha power would cut down resistance. The presence of the British altered everything. One of the Maratha leaders

74

suggested immediate withdrawal, but he was overruled. A Maratha force attacked a Rohilla fort but withdrew when British troops approached. Another, after a minor brush with the British, decided not to risk a full-scale encounter.

Nothing could have better epitomized the anarchic situation in northern India at the time than the hostilities in Rohilkhand. Shuja-ud-daulah, still the chief minister of the empire, supported by the British – legally the emperor's revenue collectors in Bengal – was ranged against an army consisting of the commander of Imperial troops, allied with agents who had been instructed by the emperor to attach the revenue of two of his provinces, which had been granted to him by the British and were part of the territory of his chief minister!

The irony, of course, was of no interest to anyone, least of all to the Marathas. They were only concerned with the realities of their situation – and they were not favourable. They did not wish to fight the British as they did not feel strong enough to guarantee the outcome in their favour. But there was also another, and possibly more pressing reason for ending the affair. News had arrived that the Maratha leader, the Peshwa, was dead and that it was in the interest of all the Maratha chiefs to be at his capital of Poona during what might be a crisis of succession. Negotiations were opened with Shuja and the British. Shuja promised to collect an indemnity from the Rohillas on behalf of the Marathas! Presumably he anticipated collecting the subsidy the Rohillas had promised him at the same time.

The withdrawal of the Marathas seemed to offer an unexpected relief to the emperor Shah Alam. He had informed the British that his handing over of Allahabad and Kora to the Marathas had been under duress. If the British would only resume the payment of his subsidy it was possible that he might be able to improve his position and even begin to assert something of the old imperial authority. Unfortunately the British attitude to the emperor could not have been cooler. Hastings saw no reason to renew an annual payment of nearly 3 million rupees, when the economy of Bengal was in a state of collapse. It was surely not his business to 'supply the pageantry of a mock king'. After the emperor's return to Delhi, the arguments against payment were even more cogent. It was unthinkable that such 'dangerous homage' should be paid while the emperor was 'the tool of the only enemies we have in India [i.e. the Marathas] and who want by such aids to prosecute their designs even to our own ruin'.

The emperor had done his best to convince the British that they should support him and that with their aid he might manage to achieve some independence of action. He had tried to bypass the British in Bengal on a number of occasions and appeal directly to the king in London. In 1766 he sent an envoy with letters and presents, but they had been intercepted by Clive who promised to deliver them himself but did not do so. Another letter in 1769, though it had been forwarded to England, had brought no reply. In 1772, after his return to Delhi and when the subsidy had suddenly and almost totally ceased, the emperor tried again. This time he appointed an Englishman as his personal envoy to King George III. The choice was unfortunate. Major John Morrison, who had joined the Bengal army in 1768, had decided that there was no longer much profit to be made there. In 1771 he left in the hope of finding employment with some Indian prince where the gleanings might be richer. Those offered by Shah Alam, now determined to return to Delhi, seemed promising, and Morrison was able to persuade the emperor that he was a man of much experience and military expertise. The news of Morrison's appointment did not please the British in Calcutta, and Hastings thought of demanding that the emperor dismiss him. But it seemed probable that Shah Alam would refuse such a demand. He had departed for Delhi without British help, and their failure to provide it still rankled. As Hastings put it in a letter to Sir Robert Barker, 'nothing exposes weakness so much as demands that cannot be enforced'. Morrison therefore continued in the emperor's employ, though in what capacity was at first somewhat obscure.

The next the British heard of Morrison was that he had been given the rank of general in the imperial forces and appointed ambassador to the Court of St James. This bombshell arrived in the form of a letter from Morrison to Warren Hastings, telling the governor of his appointment, asking whether he 'would receive him in his public character, and demanding a passage in one of the Company's ships to England'. Hastings replied that he would neither receive Morrison nor give him a passage. The imperial envoy returned Hastings's reply unopened, complaining that it had not been addressed to him by his ambassadorial rank. The governor, in turn, chose to be insulted. Who was Shah Alam to be sending ambassadors to the British, who had done so much for him and received nothing but ingratitude in return? It was, Hastings thought, all a plot to try to deprive the Company of its position in Bengal.

In view of the state of relations between the British government and the Company in England, this was not entirely irrational. The Company had powerful political and commercial enemies who would have been quite prepared to accept a grant of the revenue collection in Bengal from the emperor, and to use it as an excuse for depriving the Company of its Indian possessions by abrogating the charter on which the Company's authority depended. Hastings insisted that it was absolutely essential that the contents of the letter Morrison carried, as well as the background to his mission, should be known in England before the envoy himself reached there. It was easy enough to find out the contents of the emperor's letter, which was addressed to 'Our Brother dear to us as Life'. It offered King George III the territories now occupied by the Company. Hastings did his best to slow Morrison down by preventing him from embarking on a foreign ship. He succeeded in stopping him from travelling on a Danish vessel, but was unable to repeat this manoeuvre in the case of a Dutch ship – even though, as he complained, the Dutch customarily had a rule that foreigners were not allowed to travel to Europe in their ships.

What happened when Morrison reached England is not known, but the emperor received neither acknowledgement of, nor reply to, his letter, despite his expressed hope that the 'doors of correspondence be kept open, for the arrangement of the concerns of this World is dependent upon Friendship'.

In 1773 Hastings took the decision not only to stop the subsidy altogether – which was by then an almost academic exercise – but to return the provinces of Allahabad and Kora to Shuja-ud-daulah in exchange for a payment of 5 million rupees. This arrangement was arrived at after much bargaining at a meeting in August between Shuja and Hastings at Banaras. The principal concern of both parties was undoubtedly the preservation of Oudh. Shuja's reasons were simple, Hastings's rather more complex. For the British, Oudh was essential to the security of Bengal, but there was nothing against the British being paid to ensure it. The state of Bengal's finances was such that the economy might collapse. The consequence of such a collapse, not only for Bengal but for the British collectively and individually, could be nothing but disastrous. The Company would be at the mercy of its domestic enemies.

Such was the rationale of Hastings's thinking and it was only later that he was to be condemned for it. Hastings could have taken over the provinces of Allahabad and Kora for the Company, but they were far from the borders of Bengal, and in any case, Shuja was anxious to get them back. It was a good bargain to sell them for 5 million rupees, especially as 2 million would be in immediate cash. Hastings admitted that 'it was a very adequate compensation for a territory which perhaps ought in policy to have been given to him [Shuja], even though no return had been made for it'. But no one would have been more surprised than Shuja if he had been given back the two provinces for nothing. He would not have interpreted their return as generosity or even as justice, but as stupidity or, at best, as weakness. Such a gesture however morally admirable would have eroded the credibility of the British more than any military defeat. Lack of success in battle was a momentary misfortune, there was always another time, but softness of heart was a mortal disease in eighteenth-century India.

There was nothing soft about Hastings's heart, at least in his dealings with Indian rulers. For ordinary people his sympathy was wide and deep but he was wise in the game of princes. Everything had a price and he intended, as often as permitted, to be the one who fixed it. If Shuja wanted a British force at his disposal, it would cost him 230,000 rupees a month. Shuja was not only willing but anxious to offer an even bigger bonus: if the British would help him to annex Rohilkhand he would give them 4 million rupees over and above the expenses of the troops during the campaign. Weighing the obvious financial advantages against his general instructions from the directors not to send British troops outside Oudh, Hastings agreed – but he did not include this agreement in the official treaty. He was able to do this as his negotiations with Shuja had been carried on without witnesses. Hastings found the nawab had 'an uncommonly quick apprehension'; they understood each other and parted friends.

It had been a hard haggling and there was no doubt who had made the most profit from it. Hastings had produced cash when it was most needed and given up nothing except two provinces which it would have been difficult for them to administer profitably, and a promise of help that might not have to be fulfilled and, even if it was, would be profitable, whatever the outcome. But on one matter he had not been willing to accommodate Shuja. The nawab had wanted control of Banaras. Chait Singh, the 'raja' of that holy place, was really no more than a local landowner. His father had been a sort of ally of the British at the time of the battle of Buxar and Clive had confirmed his rather dubious title on the principle that a Hindu set between Bengal and the Muslim Shuja could do no harm and might even bring reward. Hastings confirmed the 'raja' Chait Singh in office on payment of a fixed subsidy and a feudal obligation to supply 1,000 cavalry at the Company's demand. In return, Hastings ordered all the Englishmen, except three, out of Banaras. As these had tended to dominate the trade of the area for their private profit, it was a gesture of real value to the 'raja'.

Hastings returned to Calcutta in October 1773. His Council was fully informed about the negotiations with the nawab of Oudh, including the agreement to assist him, at a price, against the Rohillas. Hastings informed the Company in London of this. He also told them that before he left Banaras, Shuja had said that he did not intend to take action against the Rohillas for the time being as he could not afford the expense. At Calcutta, Hastings justified his actions at Banaras without difficulty. He was glad that Shuja had decided against a Rohilla campaign, though he believed there were 'powerful arguments to recommend it'. As far as he was concerned, 'the sword which gave us the dominion of Bengal must be the instrument of its preservation'.

A few weeks after Hastings's return to Calcutta, Shuja demanded the fulfilment of the agreement for joint action against the Rohillas. It was tediously discussed in the Select Committee which supported it, and in the full Council which on the whole was against it. Hastings presented the case with great vigour and honesty. The Rohillas were useless as a barrier against the Marathas. The annexation of their territories by Shuja would give him a defensible frontier. The use of British troops was in the interest of the British themselves and, furthermore, Shuja would pay for them. But he did not recommend immediate compliance with Shuja's demand. For one thing, he was not convinced that the nawab would be able to fulfil the financial obligations of the agreement, and that was an essential prerequisite of British action against the Rohillas. Hastings advised that the Council should send Shuja a detailed note of the financial obligations and when they must be fulfilled. It would, Hastings believed, give Shuja an excuse for drawing back; 'that,' he said, 'I verily believe will be the issue'. He was right. Shuja dropped the project, and for the moment the British could remain 'mere watchful spectators of the distant scene'.

But not for long. Shuja knew that he could rely on British help when he finally called for it. 'My country,' he once said, 'is in reality the door of Bengal'. The call came in February 1774 and Hastings and his Council had no alternative but to answer it. Shuja had made his arrangements with considerable care. Remembering, as he did occasionally when it seemed to be to his possible advantage, that he was still nominally the emperor's chief minister, he invited Shah Alam to assist him in his campaign against the Rohillas. In the absence of the Marathas, one of the emperor's supporters, Najaf Khan, a soldier of talent, was the most powerful force in the area. Shuja would have preferred that he remain neutral, but that was too much to expect. It was better to pay for his assistance by cutting him in. Shuja therefore sent an envoy to the emperor asking for imperial troops to join the expedition and offering to divide the spoils. On the emperor's instructions, Najaf Khan met Shuja at the end of February to settle the details. Shuja gave him an extravagant welcome, for he wanted Najaf to persuade the emperor to take part in the coming campaign *in person*. This appealed to Najaf, as it meant there would always be somebody to keep an eye on Shuja and he returned to Delhi to report to Shah Alam. The idea appealed to Shah Alam, too. Though he was unwell, preparations were made for the march; but eleven days after the emperor left Delhi, on 5 April, he had to return because of the illness of his favourite son. Najaf Khan was sent on to join Shuja, but by the time he arrived at Shuja's camp, the nawab had fought his war – and won it.

It would have been more exact to say that the British had fought Shuja's war, although he had taken the profits. A brigade under Colonel Champion had been sent to assist him and, as it turned out, it was this brigade that did all the fighting. On 17 April, the British force crossed into Rohilkhand, ignoring a letter from the Rohilla leader, Hafiz Khan, suggesting an accommodation. Six days later, the two forces met in battle and the Rohillas were neatly and expeditiously cut down by disciplined artillery and musket fire. Hafiz himself was killed in the encounter.

This victory was followed by systematic and ruthless plundering on the part of Shuja's men who, according to Colonel Champion, had taken no part in the battle. Champion resented the whole affair, and complained bitterly over the brutality involved. His statements were later used against Hastings, but they reflected primarily the anger of a disappointed man. Shuja, insisting that the British had been no more than mercenaries who had already been adequately paid, maintained that they had no rights in the matter of loot. The British officers, demanding prize money, came very near to mutiny when it was refused. But the British as a power, if not as individuals, made a profit. They had moved the frontiers of the buffer state of Oudh further westwards, and had enlarged the *cordon sanitaire* between themselves and a doubtful future. Only the Rohillas really suffered, and even they regarded their defeat as the workings of an unfriendly destiny. 'The will of God is resistless' wrote Hafiz's widow. Certainly, the easy way in which the Rohillas had been swept aside seemed to confirm this estimate.

Najaf Khan viewed the matter rather differently. What he wanted, on his master's behalf – and, indirectly, on Shuja's – was half the spoils, as agreed. But Shaja maintained that the share-out had been predicated on solid aid from the emperor in person. Though the terms of the agreement had included no such proviso, the British supported Shuja, murmuring about the need to honour treaties (as if they themselves regarded all treaties as sacrosanct) while they publicly claimed that the settlement was no business of theirs. Najaf was hardly in a position to contest the issue, for the reduced force which had accompanied him would have been no match for Shuja's army. So he returned empty-handed to Delhi.

Hastings was pleased with the outcome of the campaign. He

82

believed that at least some right was on his side. Above all, he had honoured an agreement, and that in itself was a matter of great political importance. As for Colonel Champion's allegations, which would in later years be erected onto a charge of genocide, if he did not dismiss them as groundless he claimed that he could not use 'coercive power' against an ally. In any case, Champion exaggerated. Indian warfare was not the most pleasant or the most tender. Hastings ordered an enquiry to be made by Nathaniel Middleton, whom he had appointed Resident at the court of Oudh and who had been put in charge of political matters, much to Champion's resentment. Hastings demanded from Middleton the truth 'neither glossed by favour, nor blackened by prejudice'. Middleton reported that though there had been 'much distress and inconvenience', there had been no atrocities. Middleton's opinion was that the stories had been put about by members of the Company's army mainly because they had been deprived of prize money!

It was Champion's allegations which now reared their ugly heads again. On 26 October the majority in Council recalled Nathaniel Middleton. Two days later they instructed Colonel Champion to withdraw British troops helping the nawab in the pacification of Rohilkhand, though they had been primarily left there by Hastings to ensure payment of the subsidy. They also instructed Champion to demand immediate payment. Their reports to the Directors in London revealed their thinking. The Rohilla campaign had been the 'extirpation of a brave and independent nation' and ought to be enquired into by Parliament.

Colonel Champion gladly supplied sensational stories to Francis and his fellow councillors. Unfortunately, when the Council came to examine other British officers of the force sent to Rohilkhand, Champion's allegations were left unsupported. But it really did not matter. In a 'warfare of scurrility', as Hastings called it in a letter to the directors, truth was an early casualty. There was no slackening in Francis's attack. The minority imposed its own nominees for new appointments. Every form of insult was used to discredit Hastings. It was something he was not accustomed to. He sat, he said, at his Council table the 'object of the most illiberal persecution' and was 'denied even the rights of personal civility'.

Smear, innuendo, downright lies. Hastings said the declining revenue and general economic condition of the Company were due to the continuing affects of the great famine of 1770. This, said the councillors, was only a cover-up. He was corrupt; 'there is no species of peculation from which the Honourable Governor-General has thought it reasonable to abstain'. As for Barwell, he too was corrupt and no one was 'better acquainted with the great leading motive which is supposed to influence' others. Every action of the last administration, of Hastings's period of office before the Regulating Act sent these honest, reforming councillors to Bengal, was weak, improper or depraved, or all three.

Hastings was also having trouble with the Supreme Court, though as yet its actions were more of an irritation than a personal menace. The Court, Hastings wrote to Sulivan, was 'a dreadful clog on the government but I thank God the head of it is a man of sense and moderation. In all England a choice could not have been made of a man more disposed to do good and avoid mischief, which,' he added, 'is not wholly in his power and I am sorry for it'. Indeed, Impey's fellow justices seemed set on causing as much trouble as the introduction of an alien system of judicial values could make possible.

The Supreme Court had been established with the best of theoretical principles. Edmund Burke saw it as forming a 'strong and solid security for the natives against the wrongs and oppressions of British subjects resident in Bengal'. Its aim was to bring the rule of law to the Company's dominions and thus remove the lawlessness of the Company's employees. But Hastings had dreaded the effect in India of 'the complicated system of jurisprudence, the long acknowledged and lamented curse of lawyer-ridden England' and exclaimed, obviously from the heart: 'If the Lord Chief Justice and his judges should come among us with their institutes, the Lord have mercy on us'. But the Court had come and both the governor-general and the chief justice seemed powerless to stop it from interfering in areas which Hastings believed to be beyond its authority. Unfortunately, like so much in the Regulating Act, the jurisdiction of the Court was not clearly defined. The Court sent its officers to arrest important landowners and others for alleged non-payment of taxes, 'dragging the descendants of men who had once held the rights of sovereignty in this country, like felons to Calcutta, on the affidavit of a Calcutta clerk, or the complaint of a Court sergeant'. Hastings would not put up with this behaviour, and on one occasion when the Court sent a body of armed men to take over a raja's house, he sent a company of native soldiers to arrest the Court officials.

Whatever the threat to his own position, Hastings was determined to protect Indians from what a later writer was to call this 'strange tribunal' whose members knew nothing of Indian languages and customs, and which kept its records in a language known only to a few Indians. Hastings was convinced that it was better for Indians to be given justice in the terms of their traditional law, which was 'consonant to the ideas, manners, and inclinations of the people for whose use it was intended' and, because of that, 'preferable to any which even a superior wisdom could substitute'. 'The people of this country,' he maintained, 'do not require our aid to furnish them with a rule for their conduct or a standard for their property'. For the time being he could only try to minimize the impact of the Supreme Court. But it did not mean that traditional law would be abandoned. The new courts he had himself set up would continue and so would the establishment of authoritative Muslim and Hindu texts which could be translated for the use of the British who would have to administer them. One defence against the Supreme Court would turn out to be the foundation of British oriental scholarship.

In contrast to the viciousness of his opponents' correspondence with London, Hastings, though firm, was calm. Clavering he believed 'a man of strict honour, but he brought strong prejudices with him'. Monson was 'a sensible man' but just as prejudiced. As for Francis, Hastings preferred to say nothing. But he did not intend to give in to the three men. 'I shall stay out the issue of the troubles which their ill-humour, or whatever secret motive they may have, has introduced.' The secret motive was not secret for long. Hastings was soon convinced that the aim was to force him to resign or to have him removed from office. Ironically enough, whereas, before the Regulating Act, the governor could be removed by the directors at their discretion, now it was not their decision alone. Both the government and the Company had to agree, and the chances of such an agreement were small. In January 1775 Hastings decided that he must have someone he could trust in London. As his agent he sent Lachlan Macleane who had been Commissary-General since 1772, supplying him with £6,000 for his expenses on arrival in London and the promise of another £4,000 to come.

Hastings was right in thinking that his position needed defending. The councillors were roaming through all he had achieved, destroying everything they could lay their hands on. The bank he had established to stabilize the currency was abolished. His revenue regulations were condemned as 'fatal' to the economy. When Shuja-ud-daulah of Oudh died in January 1775 the majority in the Council declared Hastings's treaty of Banaras void and forced the new nawab to agree to pay a larger sum for the Company's troops quartered in his dominions. The new nawab's financial position was already serious; the subsidy was badly in arrears. Yet the councillors prevented him from receiving his full inheritance from his father's treasury. Their own man at the nawab's court, John Bristow, allowed Shuja's widows to inherit most of his wealth, ignoring Muslim law which granted them only one-eighth, and then negotiated a

86

settlement which gave the nawab a quarter of what he was entitled to. The majority also insisted that the nawab should transfer the sovereignty of the district of Banaras to the Company in return for the perpetuation of the treaty concluded with his father. Francis and his colleagues were particularly proud of this transaction. It would, they wrote, be a 'clear gain to the Company' and a great help to the declining fortunes of Bengal. And it was their sole responsibility. 'The measure is strictly and exclusively ours. The original plan was opposed in every step by the governor-general and Mr Barwell.'

Hastings and Barwell had in fact fought every step. They thought the whole business dishonourable, if not potentially dangerous, like Monson's suggestion that Rohilkhand be handed over to the emperor Shah Alam, and Clavering's that he be given back Allahabad in return for his remission of the British tribute money which Hastings had stopped paying anyway. Hastings was contemplating various plans to inhibit the freedom of action of the majority. Perhaps Lord North could be persuaded to appoint more councillors. But this would take time. Rumours had already reached him that the councillors were intriguing with certain Indians against the governor-general. What made it worse, the rumours seemed to point to Nand Kumar, one of those involved in the conspiracy that preceded Plassey, as being at the heart of the conspiracy.

The net of intrigue slowly drawing around Hastings was an immense complex of motive and personality. The manner in which the Company had acquired Bengal and the form of government that it operated meant that it was neither a British nor an Indian administration but a Eurasian one. A small number of Britons were dependent on a small number of influential Indians for the proper functioning of government. But their relationships were much more than political. Private profit could still be made only through private trade, and in this, public patronage and private enterprise were partners. The patronage was mainly British, the expertise mainly Indian, and such was the structure of profit in Bengal that any attempt at reform threatened both British and Indians. This 'establishment' was very quickly aware that the governor-general was no longer all-powerful and that it was in the interests of its members to assist the councillors in their endeavour to bring him down in disgrace.

In their efforts to insulate Hastings not only from power but from the appearance of power, the councillors had created what was almost a parallel administration dispensing patronage. Where once it had been the offices and residence of the governor-general that were crowded with petitioners of one sort or another, now many directed their attentions at those of Francis, Clavering and Monson. It was an outward sign of a sinister shift in authority. But more dangerous to Hastings were the activities of Joseph Fowke.

Fowke had once been a member of the Madras Council but he was not an ordinary merchant. Hastings believed that Fowke's hatred had been inspired by 'my not having served him to the extent of his wishes', which included a seat on the old Bengal Council. It was Fowke who introduced the sinister figure of that perennial intriguer, Nand Kumar, to Francis, but it was with Clavering that he became closest. Clavering used Fowke, though he held no official position, to investigate a case concerning a possible fraud in the salt revenue by one Kamal-ud-din and Hastings's agent, Cantoo. When Kamal complained to Hastings that Fowke had accused him of bribing members of Council, Hastings's own protest was dismissed by Francis, Clavering and Monson, who merely increased their harassment of Cantoo. Here they had a case. If it was forbidden for the native agents of collectors to farm revenues, why was the governor's allowed to, and to the extent of £100,000? Was there not a smell of corruption?

Indeed there was, and it was getting stronger. Nand Kumar inspired a complaint from the rani of Burdwan, a violent woman, whom Barwell described as 'a vile prostitute', that a number of people, including Hastings, had accepted bribes to overlook the maladministration of a guardian the Company had appointed for her son. The majority in Council welcomed this and began an investigation during which the rani produced evidence that a sum of 900,000 rupees had been distributed in bribes, including 15,000 to Hastings. But she could not produce adequate proof. In the middle of January Hastings informed Nand Kumar, 'whom, against my better nature, I have cherished like a serpent till he has stung me', that he would not be allowed into his presence again. This act of humiliation, which was made as public as possible, only incited Nand Kumar to greater efforts.

Nand Kumar was Clavering's man. Francis thought he had found someone better in Muhammed Reza Khan, who had been finally acquitted of all the charges which Hastings, under pressure from the directors and much against his will, had been compelled to bring against him. Hastings had been instructed to 'stand forth as Diwan', that is, to end Clive's dual system and take over direct rule in Bengal. Up until then, Muhammed Reza Khan had been the Company's front man, responsible for collecting the revenue. In effect, he was deputy nawab.

Hastings had no objection to removing Muhammed Reza Khan. On the contrary, he thoroughly approved of the directors' desire to end the tragic farce of dual government. But he did not approve of the arrest of the deputy nawab. It was obvious that the directors intended to make Reza Khan the scapegoat for all the troubles that had recently hit Bengal and the Company. Hastings had no alternative but to obey. On 27 April 1772 four companies of Indian troops surrounded the deputy nawab's palace at Murshidabad, and shortly afterwards Muhammed Reza Khan was on his way down-river to Calcutta under guard.

Francis assumed that Reza Khan's acquittal had been 'bought', though the deputy nawab insisted that the only present Hastings would accept was that of a Persian cat. But pressure was put upon him to change his mind and after considerable bullying and the threat of losing his property, Muhammed Reza produced the 'evidence' required.

Francis was sure that neither Hastings nor Nand Kumar knew of his relations with Muhammed Reza, but he was wrong. Francis seems to have been indiscreet on several occasions. And Hastings had the three councillors well sized up. Clavering, he complained, 'rummages' through official papers 'for disputable matters with old Fowke. Colonel Morrison receives, and I have been assured descends even to solicit, accusations. Francis writes'. Francis certainly wrote. The official minutes of the majority on the Council went back to England on every available ship. They demanded publication of their opinions on the Rohilla war. Hastings was attacked in every way from insult to apparently irrefutable accusation. And there was much appeal to principle. All bore the stamp of Francis.

Francis liked to think that he was in control of the whole situation, but it was too complicated, too stretched and irritated by personalities for that. Clavering wanted an open attack on the Supreme Court which he thought was taking on powers properly those of the Council. Chief Justice Impey was complaining to Thurlow in London that the new councillors were insolent and put on 'superior airs of authority'. Francis considered it foolish to alienate the Court as it would only drive it into support of Hastings. Francis thought Clavering unfit to succeed Hastings. Clavering was describing Francis to Lord North as a 'doubtful friend'.

Hastings's own position was dangerously exposed. He could not trust Barwell to remain on his side. He had supported Hastings over the Rohilla war and considered the actions of Francis and his colleagues 'base and infamous', but if the Cabinet in London came out against Hastings, he would surely choose the winning side. It was the only sensible thing to do. It seems too, that for a while Barwell considered marrying Clavering's daughter, Maria. This alliance would not only threaten Hastings: Francis called it a 'damnable match' – but he need not have worried. Clavering accused Barwell of corruption. Barwell called the general a scoundrel and the two men fought a duel in which the general missed and apologies were exchanged. The marriage – and the potential alliance between Clavering and Barwell – were the only casualties.

The duel between Clavering and Barwell was in the middle of May 1775; by then the other duel – between Hastings and the majority – had entered a new phase. On 11 March the majority set off the mine they and Nand Kumar had placed under the governor-general with such care and preparation. Nand Kumar had been responsible for collecting much of the material. At his house he kept court, calling to his presence land-owners, petty rajas, anyone who could conceivably be bullied or bribed into producing evidence against Hastings. There was news that a great deal of gold was changing hands and of promises of more falling thickly on Nand Kumar and the three councillors. At the Council meeting of 11 March Francis produced a sealed letter from Nand Kumar. He said he did not know what was in it, though he had his suspicions that it contained allegations against the governor-general. It did. There were accusations of corruption in association with a number of Nand Kumar's enemies, but the central charge was that Hastings had taken bribes amounting to more than 350,000 rupees from the Munny Begum (the widow of Mir Jafar), and from Nand Kumar himself!

Two days later another letter from Nand Kumar was produced stating that he had more evidence and making the request that he be allowed to present it in person. This Hastings could not allow whatever the majority might think, and they made it clear that they wanted a board of enquiry. Hastings would not be given the character of a criminal, nor would he acknowledge the three councillors as his judges. They were his real accusers. As the 'chief of this Administration, your superior, gentlemen, appointed by the Legislature itself, shall I sit . . . to be arraigned in the presence of a wretch whom you all know to be one of the basest of mankind? . . . Shall I sit to hear men collected from the dregs of the people give evidence at his dictating against my character and conduct? I will not.' When the majority voted to hear Nand Kumar, Hastings declared the Council dissolved and left the room followed by Barwell.

Clavering took the chair, maintaining that Hastings had no authority to dissolve the Council, and called Nand Kumar into the room to give his evidence. Because Nand Kumar was seventy years old, Clavering said, they would not question him too severely. In fact, none of his 'evidence' was challenged or even examined in much detail. It did not really matter. With Hastings and Barwell out of the way, the three could do as much, or as little, as they liked. Nand Kumar produced an affidavit from the Munny Begum – it was forged – but the three decided that as the seal was genuine so must be the letter to which it was attached! Without taking anyone else's evidence, the three voted Hastings guilty, and ordered him to make restitution.

Next day the rani of Burdwan's witnesses were called to give their evidence. Again Hastings dissolved the Council and again the three began to examine the witnesses after his and Barwell's departure. They called for the attendance of Cantoo but he refused to appear, as he had been instructed by Hastings. Clavering moved that Cantoo be put in the stocks, a punishment, he said, 'which the governor inflicts every day upon so many miserable Hindus merely for easing themselves upon the Esplanade'. At this Hastings threatened Clavering that if he attempted to put Cantoo in the stocks he would 'personally oppose it, at the peril of my life'. It looked as if Clavering would have to fight another duel. But he backed down.

The three did not let up on their attacks. Nand Kumar continued to supply new accusations. The three turned their inquisition into a court, demanding oaths and issuing convictions. A stream of charges was designed to put Hastings off his guard with the hope that he would lose his temper and do something which could be used against him. Hastings tried to ignore the attacks. With Barwell he was preparing a new settlement of the revenue and making proposals to Lord North for new powers for the governor-general and an amalgamation of the Company courts with the Supreme Court. His correspondence contained his justification for dissolving Council: it was 'the ancient and invariable practice of the service'. From North he required 'either my immediate recall, or . . . confirmation of the authority of which you have hitherto thought me deserving, on such a footing as shall enable me to fulfil your expectation, and to discharge the debt which I owe to your Lordship, to my country, and to my Sovereign'. If not, he would be compelled to go on being the 'idle spectator of the ruin which I cannot avert'.

For a moment, at least, Hastings considered giving up. On 27 March he wrote to Lachlan Macleane in London stating he had decided that if he heard from England that the Company and the government disapproved of his actions in the Rohilla war and of the treaty of Banaras, he would take the next available ship home: 'In that case I have nothing to hope, and shall consider myself at liberty to quit this hateful scene before my enemies gain their complete triumph over me'. They were certainly doing well. The number of accusations was steadily growing. Nand Kumar was already triumphant: 'in short,' said George Vansittart, 'old Nand Kumar has met with employers who allow full scope to his genius'. And to show their appreciation of his efforts the three councillors did him the honour of going to his house on a formal visit. 'In all the time of Nand Kumar's prosperity, in the zenith of his power,' Barwell wrote to his sister, 'never did he see so formal and ostentatious a cavalcade, nor ever had such extraordinary honours been paid him'.

Hastings made no attempt to refute the charges brought against him. The whole affair, he insisted, was not only illegal but beneath his dignity as governor-general. He was perhaps right not to reply to charges that were false, but among them was one that at least had a basis of truth: the sum he had received from the Munny Begum as 'entertainment money'. Hastings made the tactical error of not admitting he had received the money immediately the charge was made. Later it would be said that the admission had been forced from him.

The campaign against Hastings came to a head just as the worst of the hot weather hit Calcutta. Francis had been driven almost crazy by the heat of the previous hot season in a large house where he was continuously disturbed by the noise of drums and horns from a mosque next door. This time he had a house in Alipur with a garden, but though there was silence he was still oppressed by the heat and 'tormented with the bile'. Monson was ill and on more than one occasion believed to be near death. The climate had turned Clavering into an old man. Only their wives seemed to flourish, Lady Anne Monson and Mrs Clavering holding their rival salons whatever the weather. But the three men hated Calcutta, hated Bengal, hated India. They hated Indians, especially the multitudes of servants which they were compelled, for social reasons, to maintain. They hated the British because of their bad manners and infantile pursuits; skill at putting out a candle with a well-thrown bread pellet was considered a social achievement of the highest order. Above all, they felt the country itself was an enemy, its ruin part of some elemental decadence.

The climate intensified the three men's need for action. Their fingers seemed to be everywhere manipulating the strings manufactured by Nand Kumar. But all was not going well. Kamal-ud-din, under great pressure to join what was certain to be the winning side, had been persuaded to take back his allegations against Fowke and Nand Kumar and turn them into an accusation against Hastings for conspiring against Fowke! All sorts of depositions had been extracted from him and when he tried to get them back he was manhandled by Nand Kumar's servants. At last, on the advice of a friend, he went to Hastings and told him the story. Hastings sent him to Impey for an official interrogation. The judges met together and continued with their enquiries and agreed to allow Hastings and Barwell four days in which to decide whether they wished to take legal action.

Kamal, again interviewed by Hastings, stuck to his story. Nand Kumar had tried to extract false evidence from him by a mixture of threat and bribe. It did not seem a very sure case, but on 24 April Hastings and Barwell, with a great deal of hesitation, decided to prosecute Nand Kumar, his son-in-law, and Joseph Fowke, for conspiracy. The anti-Hastings faction responded immediately by standing bail for Nand Kumar, and the Board of Revenue sent out a demand for the immediate payment of sums due from Kamal. But on 6 May the whole scene was changed. One Mohan Prashad who had attempted to sue Nand Kumar in a civil action for fraud, but had, ironically enough, been blocked by Hastings himself, converted his charge into one of forgery, so transforming it from a civil case to a criminal one.

Justices Hyde and Lemaistre found the charge good in law and committed Nand Kumar for trial. Twelve days later Hastings wrote to Macleane in London telling him that he had no intention of giving up office; 'no man,' he said, 'ever saved himself by jumping out of a carriage when he was run away'. The letter contained a significant sentence that might explain his new attitude of defiance: Nand Kumar was 'in fair way to be hanged'. But the three councillors did not think so. They were very active on Nand Kumar's behalf. They questioned police and Court officials and asked Impey to give special treatment to the accused. There were even rumours in Calcutta that they would release him by force if need be, though the three quickly denied any such intention. They were also active in other, though related, areas. They sent an agent to Murshidabad to depose the Munny Begum and put Nand Kumar's son, Guru Das in her place. The Resident they dismissed, as well as Indians who were hostile to Nand Kumar.

But the actions of the three councillors antagonized the Supreme Court. Their actions were illegal. The Court was 'known and believed to be above all influence', especially from the Council, which had no authority whatsoever 'to correct or control any acts of the judges, either in or out of the Court, be those acts ever so erroneous'. All efforts were being mounted to frustrate the Court. Nand Kumar, who was not being kept in a cell but in a luxurious tent, was holding his own receptions for well-wishers and potential false witnesses. And while this was going on the administration was also in a state of civil war. Duels were threatened between members of Council. Factions in other bodies were preparing for battle. It was even suggested to Hastings by a friend in Madras that he ought to have his food tasted in case of poison.

The three were keeping their friends and the directors in London constantly informed, or misinformed, on their actions and motives. They alleged that Nand Kumar was in danger of assassination as he 'was the principal evidence against the governor-general'. Francis wrote to Clive – he had not heard that Clive had committed suicide nearly six months before – that the persecution of Nand Kumar actually validated the charges he had made against Hastings! But all this did not help Nand Kumar. He was no longer in his comfortable tent but in the common jail and his trial was about to take place.

The trial opened on 8 June. The four judges sat on the bench; the jury was composed entirely of Englishmen. The case lasted for eight days, the court sitting from early in the morning to late at night. The evidence given was complex. There were masses of documents in Persian, and other languages, but none in English. Oral evidence had to be laboriously translated. The jury had no doubts about Nand Kumar's guilt. Even Chambers, a friend of Francis and sympathetic to the accused, stated later that 'he was certainly guilty of uttering the writing in question, knowing it to be forged'. The judges sentenced him to be hanged, for this was British law. Indian law was much more lenient on matters of forgery.

The verdict came as a shock, to the three councillors and to the people of Bengal. But Nand Kumar believed there was still the chance of reprieve. The governor-general had the authority, and if he failed to act, Francis, Clavering and Monson could exercise clemency for him. But there was to be no reprieve. Hastings refused. So, surprisingly, did the others, rejecting an appeal from

Nand Kumar. The day before the execution, Clavering received another appeal but did not open the document containing it until ten days later at a meeting of Council where it was unanimously condemned as a libel on the judges of the Supreme Court. On 5 August Nand Kumar was hanged and his body was taken away to be burned by members of his own caste, the Brahmins. It was a significant act in many senses. No one in Bengal doubted that he had died because he had attacked Hastings. It was obviously unwise, however high your social status and however influential your British friends might be, to take on the governor-general.

The charge against Nand Kumar was proved and only the sentence is open to criticism. It was certainly unjust, and that Hastings allowed it to stand was demonstrably against his own opinions about the relevance of British law to Indian circumstances. There is no question – though it has been argued on and off over the years since his death – that the execution of Nand Kumar was a judicial murder and that Hastings' acquiescence in it was an act of self-defence and no more. Nand Kumar would in time return to haunt him, but at the moment there were other, more pressing problems.

It was not until June 1775 that news of the conflict between Hastings and his Council reached London. There was talk of recalling Hastings but other problems were tormenting king and Parliament. As one Welbore Ellis reported to Francis the 'state of the American Colonies and the constant fatiguing attendance and mass of business in Parliament have driven all consideration of your matters out of doors'.

Soon it began to appear, as Richard Palk wrote to Hastings in the middle of November 1775, that the government had no desire 'to be further embarrassed with disputes in India, nor are they very anxious to vindicate your opponents further than what men will naturally do to justify their own nomination.'

The only consequence was a general letter from the directors sent off in December containing a mixture of censure and praise for everyone and an appeal to all to work together in some sort of harmony! The letter arrived in June 1776. Hastings believed his actions had been condemned without justification, but he had no intention of sending in his resignation. It was just as well, for August brought news from England that when the directors by a one-vote majority had decided to recall both Hastings and Barwell, a meeting of stockholders had reversed the decision by the substantial majority of 107. To Francis this was a heavy blow, especially as both Clavering and Monson were forced by illness to stay away from meetings of Council. In August Monson sent in his resignation; and early in September, tormented by boils, so did Clavering, though he told no one, not even Francis. On 25 September, the majority disappeared. Monson was dead, and that same afternoon buried. Hastings now held the majority with Barwell, and his casting vote. But it was a situation that could not last for long. Monson would certainly be replaced. In fact it was what was happening in London rather than in Bengal that would decide Hastings's future.

Back in England news that the anti-Hastings group in the Council were encouraging Nand Kumar to produce evidence against the governor-general, frightened the nabobs. Who could know what sort of evidence, even truthful evidence, might emerge to discredit them? The nabobs came together to protect themselves, and their coalition was formidable, both in the Company and in Parliament. In the House many of them were from the Opposition, even though most had no particular friendship for Hastings or for Lawrence Sulivan, who still supported the governor-general. Hastings's agent Lachlan Macleane was reluctant to come out on the side of the nabobs until he had explored every possible avenue of approach to the government. It was only after there turned out to be none that he gave his support to the Opposition. These now declared themselves against 'the cruel treatment of the best servants the Company ever had abroad'. The intrigues did, however, stimulate an anti-Hastings vote in the General Court of the

Company, but as it was by show of hands, a ballot was demanded which resulted in a substantial majority of 377 to 271 for giving further consideration to the resolution.

When this information reached Calcutta, Francis was incensed. 'Mr Hastings,' he wrote, 'with an air that would become Cato the Censor, declares that for his part he is satisfied with the absolution given him by 377 plain, honest men, obtained without influence or intrigue and extorted by the force of truth in opposition to the whole power of the Ministry . . . Such impudence is a vomit for a dog.' It did not alter the fact that whatever the vote for the piper, the government called the tune. Lord North declared he would 'have nothing to do with India matters out of Parliament', and made it clear that whatever happened in the Company, he would use Parliament to remove Hastings and Barwell.

Francis continued to send back to England a wide range of smears. While the British were losing the American colonies, he reported that Hastings rejoiced at British defeats. Hastings was sending money home through the Dutch and planning to escape justice and live in Switzerland on his ill-gotten gains. Hastings's dismissals of Bristow, Fowke and others were unjust and spiteful and really designed to hurt him and Clavering. In Council Francis would appear to support a proposal and then destroy its validity in a torrent of rhetorical analysis. An attack withdrawn in Calcutta would be published in full in London. It was siege warfare that had to be contended with on a multiplicity of fronts. No wonder Francis prided himself on being able to drive Hastings 'to a degree of madness'. What he most hoped for was to drive Hastings into resignation. In June 1777 it looked as if he had succeeded, for on the 19th, despatches from the directors were opened and read in Council. From them they learned that the governor-general's resignation had been accepted and that Edward Wheler, an ex-chairman of the Company, had been appointed in his place.

Shock and indignation were Hastings's immediate responses

to the directors' despatches, not so much to the fact of his recall –
that had always been a very real possibility – but to the
acceptance of his 'resignation'. What resignation? He had not
resigned or authorized anyone to offer resignation on his behalf.
The only explanation must be that those he had trusted with
looking after his interests in London had turned on him and
joined his enemies. It was to be some time before he learned what
had actually happened.

Lachlan Macleane, whom Hastings had appointed as his
agent in London, reached England in 1775, as did another friend,
John Graham, whom Hastings asked to assist Macleane. In the
following year Hastings's old friend George Vansittart arrived
with masses of documents in support of Hastings's case against
the accusations of Francis, Clavering and Monson. The instructions Hastings had given Macleane on his leaving Bengal were to
be the subject of controversy, but there is no doubt that Hastings
had given him and Graham 'unlimited discretion to act for me as
they thought best'. He had also made it quite clear to Macleane,
Graham and Vansittart that he would not allow himself to be
recalled, and should it seem that the government was determined
on dismissing him, he would prefer to be given the opportunity
of resigning.

Macleane appeared, from the first, to have been an excellent
choice to press Hastings's case and interests. He had many
friends, was a fluent speaker and was anything but lazy in spite of
weak lungs. Lawrence Sulivan maintained that it was Macleane's superb handling and eloquent advocacy that had made
the stockholders reverse the directors' decision to recall Hastings
and Barwell. But Sykes warned Hastings that he did not think
Macleane would 'in the end . . . do you much good'. In fact,
Macleane was not trusted by men of substance. Even his praise
by Sulivan was merely the praise of a bankrupt, not the best of
references. Macleane was also involved in the debt that
enmeshed the nawab of Arcot. He also had ambitions, grandiose
ambitions. He wanted to acquire all the East India Company's

stock for himself!

Sulivan claimed that the overwhelming majority for Hastings had been a triumph for Macleane, but had it? Certainly he had done much of the organizing, but the real vote was not for Hastings but the product of a wide, and by no means harmonious, spectrum of motives. Worse still, the government had taken the vote as a direct flouting of its wishes and there were rumours spreading about that Lord North contemplated bringing the affairs of the Company and of Bengal before Parliament once again. Not only that, but North's secretary, John Robinson, who was the filter through which most information passed to his chief, was preparing a memorandum for Barwell. Faced, he thought, with a determined bid to dispose of Hastings, Macleane, in spite of the fact that he was in possession of a letter from Hastings in which he stated that he had no intention of resigning until he heard the outcome of the various moves against him in London, felt that his only course of action might well be to offer Hastings's resignation.

Very soon Alexander Eliot, a protégé of Hastings in his first governorship in Bengal and son of Sir Gilbert who would one day be among the managers of Hastings's impeachment, approached Macleane with an offer from Lord North. This was early in August 1776. By October the negotiations had led to an agreement that would provide for 'retreat with honour'. Macleane asked for some sort of reward for Hastings, a peerage perhaps, but that was not immediately acceptable because it would look too much like a bribe. Macleane's other terms, which he had discussed with Sulivan, Vansittart and other friends of Hastings, were agreed to. Those who had been dismissed from their appointments by the majority in the Bengal Council, both British and Indian, would be restored if not to the actual office they had been deprived of, at least to one of equal or near-equal status. Hastings would be given a formal reception on his return to London and there would be no recriminations of any sort.

By the middle of October all was over. The directors had accepted Macleane's authority to act on behalf of Hastings. Vansittart and another friend of Hastings, John Stewart, testified to that authority. Macleane offered Hastings's resignation. It was accepted and Edward Wheler was appointed in his place. Sulivan, at least, was more than satisfied: 'the battle,' he wrote off to Hastings, 'is at last ended with every mark of respect'. It came as something of a shock when a month later it was announced that Clavering had been knighted with the honour of the Order of the Bath. Macleane wrote off to Hastings advising him not to resign. The agreement, at least in spirit, had been broken by the elevation of Clavering. At the same time Macleane began to offer excuses for his actions, not overtly but by suggestion. Lord North, he said, had not really believed in Hastings's resignation. As proof he offered the fact that when the news of Monson's death reached London, the prime minister had changed Wheler's appointment from governor-general to that of councillor in succession to Monson. What that meant was that the senior councillor in Bengal would succeed Hastings – and he was Clavering.

When the despatches from the directors had been read in Council, Hastings adjourned the meeting. Hastings and Barwell returned to Government House where Barwell decided to stay in rooms prepared for him. The two men consulted on what action Hastings should take. It seems that they agreed that despite Hastings's withdrawal of his offer to resign he should not resist the decision of the government. Barwell wrote to his sister that Hastings had decided to give up office 'as a healing and conciliating measure'. In the meantime and until the arrival of Edward Wheler, it would have to be business as usual. Hastings therefore called a meeting of the Board of Revenue, on which the councillors sat, for the following day. While on his way to the meeting, Barwell received an order from Clavering, as acting governor-general, to attend a council meeting at eleven o'clock that morning.

Barwell immediately went to Hastings, and as the two men were discussing Clavering's actions, a note was delivered addressed to Warren Hastings Esq., demanding that he give up the keys to the fort and the treasury not later than noon. Francis, it appeared, had tried to dissuade Clavering from what Barwell described as 'a provocation of . . . great magnitude', but Clavering, hot-tempered, sickly, determined at last to be governor-general come what may, would not be restrained. Hastings had resigned, the despatches said so, he was the senior councillor, he must succeed. But Hastings was even more determined that he should not. Forgotten was his decision to accept the instruction of the directors even though it had been based upon a misunderstanding. Clavering would not, must not, be allowed to assume office.

Hastings immediately sent orders to the officers commanding at Fort William and at the depot at Barrackpur outside Calcutta, that they must accept no orders but his. Hastings then called the justices of the Supreme Court to meet at the Council House and pass judgement on Clavering's action. Hastings would abide by their decision; was Clavering prepared to do the same? Yes, but only after Francis had, with some difficulty, persuaded him that he must have the appearance of legality on his side. Through the night the justices examined the evidence before them and finally at four o'clock in the morning gave their decision, and it was unanimous. Clavering had usurped office. Hastings had not legally resigned or vacated his post. Would Clavering accept? Not immediately, he needed time to think. And while he did, rumour poured through the bazaars, washed against the fine houses of the British and the mini-palaces of rich Bengalis and flowed into the countryside where the parched earth of the friends of Francis and Clavering received it as a refreshing stream. But at noon, Clavering accepted the Court's decision.

All was not yet over. Two days later Hastings summoned a meeting of Council but sent the summons only to Barwell. At this meeting they decided that Clavering had by his actions forfeited his seat on the Council and his post of commander-in-chief by assuming the office of governor-general. Clavering took his case to the Supreme Court, which with ostentatious neutrality declared that it was a matter for decision by higher authority in London. At a meeting held on 25 June at which Francis and Clavering were present, the Council decided to accept this compromise, Francis claiming the role of mediator. In his letters home he said that he thought Hastings, Barwell and Clavering must all be recalled. That only left Francis. So sure was he of his claim that he declared that he would consider the appointment of anyone else to the office of governor-general as his own dismissal.

The same vessel that took Francis's claim to the succession – and his threat – carried Hastings's own letters to Lord North. Only Clavering's outrageous actions had stopped him from resigning office; in the circumstances he felt it his duty to stay at his post, particularly as he could not believe that 'your Lordship could have made an accommodation of peace the lure to drag me into the power of my most rancorous enemy, and to make me sacrifice to the most brutal outrage and indignity'. It was quite impossible for him to accept that his 'lordship should expect from me tame submission to such treatment'. He could not hope to be 'confirmed in this government' but neither would he expect to be 'dragged from it like a felon'. To his friends Hastings claimed that he had always intended to resign only when *he* decided that it was the proper moment to do so.

As time passed, Clavering began to regret that he had given in to Hastings and the Supreme Court. He had invested himself with the red ribbon of the Order of the Bath and was now Sir John, beloved of the king, and was writing to everyone in any sort of authority in and around the Company's dominions in India drumming up support. Even Barwell was beginning to wonder what could happen next in this extraordinary situation. He might have a chance at the office of governor-general himself, though he would never join with Clavering and Francis to drive

Hastings 'from his station'. If he did it would 'brand me with infamy'. Against his advice Hastings sent off an indignant letter to the directors. Macleane had no authority to offer his resignation nor had he given Vansittart and Stewart any right to testify.

Hastings had something much more effective than words, or even truth, on his side. The sceptical would say that it was the debilitating climate of Calcutta, built on a swamp, divided by open drains, a hothouse of disease. The people of Bengal thought Hastings was blessed with luck, potent and magical. On a Saturday in the Indian month of Bhadras (15 August – 15 September) Nand Kumar had been executed, and Colonel Monson had joined his wife in South Park Street cemetery. On Saturday, 30 August, Sir John Clavering KCB died, hostile to the last, giving strict orders that Hastings should not be informed of his death until he had been put in his grave!

All these events were taking place in a semi-vacuum. The time differential between Britain and India, a variable one of anything up to six months or longer for letters to get from one place to the other, imposed a vital discontinuity between decision and events, resembling a slip between soundtrack and image on a movie film.

As soon as Clavering was dead Francis was pleading his case with Lord North. Surely Hastings and Barwell must be recalled? Surely he, Francis, should succeed? 'Three years' incessant application have made me a tolerable master of affairs. In a much shorter time I do not think it possible for any man with whatever abilities, to qualify for the conduct of them.' Lord North remained unimpressed. There was no political profit to be made out of appointing Francis governor-general. Francis thought that his position was being undermined by North's secretary, John Robinson; that 'treacherous scoundrel', Francis called him privately to his own friends.

For Edmund Burke, Francis took a somewhat different line. 'Whatever your idea of political characters in England, you have men to contend with at the worst, and many of them honourable – but these are devils . . . You and I, Sir, seem to be travelling up opposite sides of a steep hill – but I hope we shall meet near the top of it. It is reserved for us, I trust, to look back from stations not too widely separated, to the weary steps we have taken – to compare the difficulties we have surmounted, and to descend into the Vale of Life together.'

Francis also took the precaution of sending a letter to Madras to await the arrival of Edward Wheler, warning him to have nothing to do with Hastings or Barwell until Francis had given him the facts.

Wheler arrived at Calcutta on 11 December. He had expected to find Clavering alive, and he was not quite sure of his own position. Hastings tried to identify it for him. He sent Alexander Elliot, who had returned to Bengal just before Wheler, to offer the governor's terms. Hastings demanded Wheler's neutrality and to ensure it was prepared to make one concession to Francis: he would allow him a share in the appointment of officials. But he wanted Muhammad Reza Khan dismissed and the present revenue settlement extended for another two years. Francis handled Wheler better than Elliot. Wheler would not commit himself but only promise to view every matter on its individual merits 'without regard to persons or parties'. When Council met on 30 December Wheler voted against every one of Hastings's proposals. All Hastings required would have to be authorized by the use of his casting vote.

This, in fact, was how it was done, though not without a running battle of bickering over petty detail. Francis continued his smear campaign and was pleased that everything that came out of London was hostile to Hastings. Instructions arrived for the restoration of Bristow at Lucknow and condemnation for the revenue commission as a waste of money. Hastings found the directors' letters 'studiously abusive'. But Sulivan, at least, felt that events were on the side of Hastings. In the autumn of 1777, General Burgoyne was forced to surrender to American rebels at

Saratoga. That news arrived in Calcutta in June 1778. It was followed a month later by the information that France and Britain were at war. 'Who in such a crisis,' wrote Sulivan, 'would they dare put in your place?'

At this time Hastings was faced with a conspiracy between the French and the Marathas. He was convinced that the real threat to the British presence in India would come from the activities of the French in alliance with native powers. The war with France would undoubtedly spread to India; already there were French ships off the Malabar coast. It was absolutely essential to establish 'a firm interest in the most powerful state in India [i.e. the Marathas], and check in its first growth the seeds which the French have sown of an alliance with it, and, which if suffered to grow to maturity, may prove fatal to the British possessions in India'.

When the news from America and of the outbreak of war with France arrived, Hastings's reaction offended Francis. 'Hastings and almost everybody here is in high triumph,' he noted. 'They seem to consider their own security as united with the ruin of the Empire.' Francis saw affairs outside India as a sign for retrenchment and defence, Hastings saw them as an imperative for further action. Retreat would be carefully noted by Indian rulers and give the French the best of arguments: 'if it really be true that the British arms and influence have suffered a severe check in the Western world, it is more incumbent on those who are charged with the interest of Great Britain in the East to exert themselves for the retrieval of the national loss'.

While Hastings was talking of patriotic war, Francis, in the interest of undermining Hastings personally, was leaking documents from the directors criticizing him, not only to members of the Company's service in Bengal and elsewhere, but to interested Indians, including the emperor Shah Alam. And what did that amount to but 'an invitation to place no confidence in the present government and to its subjects to disobey its authority?' It was, Hastings maintained, a sort of treason, and one very difficult to suppress. It could indeed, only be answered by a demonstration of strength and decisiveness. And against the French. All that was needed was success. With it, all the intrigues of Francis, the hostility of the directors and of all his enemies would be blown away in a whirlwind of gratitude.

Hastings got his success though a somewhat conditional one. The French were put in their place by the occupation of the enclave of Chandernagar near Calcutta, and Bombay was saved from the Marathas by a most spectacular march across India by a Company's force out of Bombay, led by Colonel Goddard. But this was only after a British force had surrendered to the Marathas and agreed the terms of an humiliating treaty, immediately repudiated by Hastings.

Just at the moment when Hastings needed all his power in Council, his position was almost undermined – by a friend. At the end of 1778 Barwell told Hastings that he would leave India. He was rich, his ambition to become governor-general was unlikely to be fulfilled, his friends were pressing him to return to England and his young wife was dead: there was nothing to keep him in Calcutta. And yet there was. Barwell, indolent, pleasure-loving, responded to Hastings's appeal, made in open Council, with the sneers of Francis dirtying the air, and put friendship and what he conceived as his duty, first. He would stay until his presence on the Council was no longer essential.

But it was possible that even with Barwell willing to stay Hastings would no longer be in control. The Council was short of one member since the death of Clavering, and the man appointed in his place was someone Hastings thoroughly disliked. In fact, when Eyre Coote had left India seven years before, Hastings had written to Sulivan: 'may success and honour attend him in any other part of the world, but God forbid that he should ever return to any part of India again'. Now Coote was to come back to Bengal as commander-in-chief, and as a member of Council. As a soldier and nothing more, Coote was tolerable. Though orthodox in his military thinking he had the vital ability to attract devotion from his men. The native soldiers would follow him anywhere. But Coote would not – as a member of Council – be restricted to military matters. His political opinions were naive, his tact and diplomacy non-existent. He was prickly about status, quarrelsome about most things and foul-tempered. He distrusted civilians and was quick to take offence at any suggestion real or imagined, of civilian control of the army. Coote had three fundamental weaknesses: he could be easily flattered, he liked his opinions to be listened to with respect, and he loved money.

From friends in England, Hastings heard that Coote would certainly give him his support, and its continuance could be ensured by the right sort of sweetening. Hastings took the hint and indeed went so far in satisfying Coote that the action he took became one of the charges of impeachment. Coote was to have a large estate which until recently had belonged to the Governor of Chandernagar, and very substantial field allowances, which were assumed to start the moment he set foot in Bengal. On his arrival he was received with considerable display and assured by Hastings that there would be no interference in military matters. Though in Madras, while on his way to Bengal, Coote had criticized both Bombay and Hastings over the Maratha war, in Council in Calcutta he voted with Barwell and Hastings for the latter's plan of campaign. Coote also voted with the governor-general on other matters. Francis, wrote Hastings, 'is miserable and is weak enough to declare it in a manner much resembling the impatience of a passionate woman, whose hands are held to prevent her doing mischief'. Not that it prevented Francis from trying. He was perpetually filling Coote's ear with scandal and smear, until Coote could stand it no longer and took himself off to join the army. Francis had lost a potential ally, but not altogether, for once in camp Coote began to dissent from Hastings's judgements.

Hastings's relations with the directors in London were still no smoother. The period covered by the Regulating Act was coming to an end, and though it was believed that there would be no change in Hastings's position there was no positive evidence. When the Act expired in October 1779 nothing had been heard in Calcutta. The despatches that did arrive were almost always critical of the governor-general; what they would be like when they heard of the Maratha war could safely be predicted. Hastings was convinced that whatever he did would be condemned. The directors ordered him to reinstate Francis's friends Fowke and Bristow and Muhammed Reza Khan as well. This Hastings refused to do. 'When they [the directors] abandon the line of their duty, leave me uninstructed upon every point of business, and fill all their letters, which are volumes, with gross invectives against me, and with orders which have no object but to gratify partial favour and personal rancour, they forfeit their title to my obedience.' At last, in November, news came that the Regulating Act would remain in force for another year. No change, no relief from conflict and criticism.

But change was to be forced on Hastings. Early in 1780 Barwell told Hastings he would stay no longer. Barwell's decision coincided with the breakdown of negotiations between Goddard and the Marathas and war again.

The loss of Barwell and the renewal of war in the west were part of the interest on a growing capital of menace. Late in 1779 there was authentic proof, sent by Goddard, that Mysore, Hyderabad and the Marathas were virtually in alliance against the British. Where the blow would fall first was still no more than a guess, but the British in Madras seemed to be determined that it should be there in the south. The governor, Sir Thomas Rumbold, blundered from one inept and needless provocation to another without, apparently, any thought for the consequences. And Rumbold had once been in the running for the office of governor-general! Rumbold angered the ruler of the Deccan, but, more seriously still, seemed to go out of his way to offend Haidar Ali of Mysore. At one time Rumbold suggested an alliance with Mysore, and a couple of months later, an attack on

Mysore from Madras, Bombay and Bengal! Yet there was little Hastings could do. He did not have the power to crush Rumbold and discipline Bombay. His dilemma was that he would 'not stay longer if I am left in the same impotent and distressed state', nor would he 'leave this country, if I have an option, to the mercy of Philip Francis'. How he was 'to reconcile these dissimilar resolutions' he could not yet tell. Yet, by February 1780 the reconciliation seemed to have been achieved. Hastings and Francis had come to terms!

The pressures that drove the two men into even the most fragile of alliances were real and powerful. For Hastings the exterior menace to British India was compounded by the interior menace to his government in Bengal. Not only were there the steady rancours of the Council but the governor-general was having serious difficulties with the judges of the Supreme Court, difficulties which threatened the fundamental workings of the administration. As for Francis, the only motive that can be disentangled from his letters and private journals seems quite simply to have been to take advantage of the situation and to get his own price for his cooperation – a most powerful motive indeed.

In his journal and letters Francis constructs a fantasy. 'The British empire in India is tottering', and any accommodation with Hastings is 'on public ground and no other' and only in the hope of preventing 'more mischief'. As for the possibility of some arrangement between the French and the Marathas, it was no more than illusion. There were certainly no concessions to Hastings, 'that man of microscopic sagacity'. Their compromise was no more than sound strategy.

There were a number of intermediaries between the two men, the last being John Day, the Attorney-General, once a Francis man but now something of an admirer of Hastings. In February 1780 Mrs Hastings gave a dinner. Francis noted in his journal that it was 'a pacific dinner' and three days later, on 7 February, the terms of accommodation between the enemies were agreed.

There was nothing in writing, no formal, and therefore quotable, agreement. Hastings in a moment of innocence believed that Francis could be trusted. Perhaps he thought that when the options faded patriotism was all, that 'honour', that eighteenth-century paradigm, exorcized ambition – and destroyed the past. He could not know – though he should have guessed – that Francis at this moment of apparent reconciliation was writing to his friends, 'When I speak of pacification with Mr Hastings I mean literally what I say. It is *not* union. It is *not* alliance . . . In short, it is more like an armed truce than like anything else'.

Hastings really believed in Francis's public image. So did Richard Barwell, for there is little doubt that he would have stayed in India if he had not. Perhaps he thought that the price Hastings had paid was sufficient, even for Francis. In return for an agreement by Francis not to oppose anything the governor-general decided was best for the prosecution of the war against the Marathas or 'for the general support of the present political system', Francis was offered a number of concessions. Fowke would go back to Banaras, Muhammed Reza Khan would be reinstated, and a number of minor Francis supporters would be given lucrative appointments. Hastings may well have thought of the arrangement as a calculated risk. 'I regard it,' he wrote later, 'as a deed of faith and honour not of law . . .' Any risk, perhaps, was worth taking when the whole of British dominion in India was threatened. And for a while at least the agreement seemed to work.

Hastings had made his arrangement with Francis basically for one reason only, freedom in the control of the Maratha war. For a while it seemed that freedom was there. Goddard was doing extremely well in Gujarat. In the small state of Gohad, on the western frontier of Oudh, Major Popham, sent by Goddard to clear it of the Marathas, had been successful. Hastings then planned something larger – and more impressive. On 12 June he proposed in Council that a force should be sent to invade the territories of the Maratha leader Mahadaji Sindia and attack his capital at Gwalior. This Hastings thought would divert the Maharathas to such an extent that Goddard would not only be relieved of pressure but could move with some effect against Poona the Maratha capital. It was, Hastings was convinced, a decisive move and he was prepared to plead in Council for its implementation.

But Francis, with the support of Wheler, would have none of it; it would cost too much, the season was wrong, the army would find itself defeated in the harsh wastes of central India. Hastings replied that this was the most abject defeatism. 'Acts that proclaim confidence and a determined spirit in the hour of adversity are the surest means of retrieving it.' Hastings even offered to pay for the expense of the force to attack Gwalior. The money would come from an attempted bribe by Chait Singh of Banaras which Hastings had paid into the Company's treasury and now saw good cause to spend. Francis, however, was not prepared to honour any agreement with Hastings unless it served his own very well-defined interests. As with any arrangement between antagonists in which the terms are not precisely and unequivocally stated in writing, each side had its own, and inevitably contradictory, interpretation. Hastings believed that Francis had agreed to support the war in western India unconditionally. 'My security was in his honour.' But that honour appeared to be flexible.

Recognizing his error, Hastings determined upon a course of action and 'in continual debate with myself concerning the manner of noticing and defeating Mr F's opposition' decided that Francis must be disposed of, once and for all. Literally so, for Hastings had decided to kill Francis. It was to be no assassination, though one could have been bought and arranged without a great deal of trouble in the Bengal of the time. Nor was it to be a judicial murder, like that of Nand Kumar. Even if Hastings considered the latter course, and it is highly unlikely that he did, there was no conceivable way in which it could have

113

been organized. But there was another way. Francis could be provoked into a duel. If he was killed by Hastings all was well, a matter of honour had been settled in an honourable manner, at least for gentlemen at that period of the eighteenth century. And if Hastings was killed? Well, he was certain that Francis, having killed a governor-general, was unlikely to take his place.

It was a strange, almost unacceptable, decision on Hastings's part. It has overtones of madness but there is little doubt that that the plan of provocation and the assessment of its consequences were made in cold blood. It was essential that everything be done publicly while the true purpose remained secret, or at least as secret as possible. Only two people, Hastings's secretaries, knew of his decision. There would be a formal statement made in Council accusing Francis of dishonourable conduct. Hastings was prepared for compromise as he believed that the British presence in India was in great danger. He informed Francis that he was prepared to take the sole responsibility for military decisions in western India and claimed the right to carry out his decisions without public obstruction. This Francis would not allow; he must see the whole plan of campaign first. Hastings determined to act; his formal statement against Francis would be given in Council on 3 July.

John Day, who had mediated the now dead agreement between Hastings and Francis, asked for the opportunity to resurrect it. Hastings was willing, and Day saw Francis at his Calcutta home on 2 July. The first response to Day's intervention was that Francis suggested that the force marching against Sindia should be halted until despatches from London had been received. This was not acceptable to Hastings. The next day, Francis was crushed by fever and was prepared to let Hastings do what he pleased. That evening Hastings issued orders for the force commanded by Major Carnac to continue its march. But he wanted more from Francis: the minutes condemning his policy must be withdrawn. On 7 July Day informed the governor-general of Francis's agreement. The minutes were withdrawn in Council the same day and Hastings went off to join his wife on board a yacht anchored off Chandernagare.

On his return to Calcutta, Hastings continued with Council meetings, none of which were attended by Francis who had left Calcutta for the country to recover from his fever – and to carry on his intrigues. Hastings heard that he was proposing to meet Coote, no doubt in an attempt at reconciliation. On July 17 Hastings was informed that Francis repudiated Day's message that he had agreed to the withdrawal of the offending minutes. The agreement, he said, had been conditional on the halting of Carnac's force. Again Day went off to find Francis, but failed. At this stage Hastings decided to put his plan of provocation into action.

On 14 August, hearing that Francis had returned to Calcutta, Hastings left the Dutch settlement of Chinsura where he had been staying with his wife, and that evening sent Francis a copy of his minute attacking his conduct. The minute had been carefully and offensively worded. 'I did hope that the intimation contained in my last minute would have awakened in Mr Francis's breast, if it were susceptible to such sensations, a consciousness of the faithless part which he was acting towards me . . . my objections do not lie in the special matter of his minutes . . . but to the spirit of opposition which dictated them. I have a right to his implicit acquiescence . . . I do not trust his promise of candour, convinced that he is incapable of it . . . Every fabricated tale of armies devoted to famine or to massacre have found their first and ready way to his office, where it was known they would meet with the most welcome reception. I judge of his public conduct by my experience of his private, which I have found to be void of truth and honour . . .'

The next day, after a meeting of the Board of Revenue, Francis asked to speak with Hastings in private. When they were alone Francis read a few lines from a paper to the effect that he would produce a formal reply to the governor-general's charges but 'no answer I can give to the matter of that paper can be adequate to the dishonour you have offered me'. Hastings replied that he 'had expected the demand and was ready to answer it'. The meeting was fixed for two days later.

The two men spent the time putting their affairs in order, Francis 'burning papers etc. in case of the worst', Hastings writing a new will, a memorandum of government business to his secretary and a letter for his wife to be given to her should he be killed. The two men met at Alipur at 5.30 in the morning of 17 August. There was some difficulty in finding a quiet spot, as even at that hour they were followed by a small mob of inquisitive Indians. Neither man had ever fought a duel before or even fired a pistol more than once or twice. But they did not seem worried. Hastings's second recorded that his principal was in 'a state of such perfect tranquility that a spectator would not have supposed that he was about an action out of the common course of things.'

At fourteen paces the two men faced each other. Hastings was determined not to fire first, but after Francis's pistol had misfired twice he took careful aim and hit his opponent at the moment Francis's pistol fired. Francis fell. 'I thought that my backbone was broke,' he wrote later in the day, and at the moment of impact he called out: 'I am dead'. Hastings's response was 'Good God, I hope not', but the wound was not mortal and Francis was able to sit up and shake hands with the victor. A stretcher was found and he was first taken to the nearest house while Hastings rode back to Calcutta to send his own doctor and the surgeon-general. The wound turned out to be clean, the ball having missed any vital part and lodged in the shoulder, but until Francis recovered Hastings remained in the capital.

'I am *well* and *unhurt*,' he wrote his wife telling of the duel. 'But you must be content to *hear* this good of me; you cannot see me. I cannot leave Calcutta while Mr Francis is in any danger.' In fact he had informed the Chief Justice of the duel and told him that if the wound proved fatal he would surrender himself so that 'the law might take its course'. That same evening he was able to write to his wife that Francis would recover. That was some relief but, he wrote, 'As you say, "Who knows what may happen; who can look into the Seeds of Time?"'

Much was happening – and quickly. The duel with Francis, very satisfactory in its outcome, was followed a few days later by the news that Popham had captured Sindia's capital of Gwalior, the 'key to Hindustan', Hastings called it. Goddard, too, was doing well in Gujarat and the disgrace of previous defeat dissolved in a new upsurge of British prestige. But just as everything seemed set for a decisive defeat of the Marathas the grand confederacy of the nizam of Hyderabad the ruler of the Deccan the Marathas Sindia and Holkar, the raja of Berar and Haidar Ali of Mysore, broke into offensive action. There was a threatened invasion from Berar; most menacing of all, there were terrifying rumours from the south. On 20 September the rumours were confirmed: Haidar Ali had destroyed an army sent against him from Madras.

At least Hastings would now be free to deal with the crisis in his own way. Though Francis was back at Council meetings within a month of the duel, by early October his resignation was on its way to the directors. After the duel Hastings had enquired whether he might visit Francis but the offer was declined. Francis would only talk to Hastings in Council. When he did so it was to present his refutation of the charges brought against him by the governor-general. The old Francis seemed to be still very active. He voted against sending money and men to Madras. He called for the end of the Maratha campaign at any price. In alliance with Coote, who had returned to take his seat on the Council, he got the scoundrelly Bristow back into the Residency in Oudh. Hastings could do nothing to prevent it and it seems that he suddenly realized that the duel, while settling Francis's fate in India, might only have released him into greater and more effective viciousness in Britain. He sent off a friend immediately to London to arrive before Francis and see that Hastings's case did not go by default and that any charge from Francis could be countered. He also chose as his agent in London Major Scott, who was to leave in January 1781.

Francis was already preparing the next stage of his own campaign against Hastings. His letter of resignation was full of reproaches. The directors had 'deceived, deserted, sacrificed and betrayed' him. Instead of backing Sir John Clavering and himself, they had insisted on keeping in office a man who took no notice of their orders. The British were now threatened on all sides; 'the empire in India is tottering to its foundation' in spite of everything he had done to save it. 'The moment I shall have made my exit, enter desolation.' Because Wheler and Coote generally supported Hastings, they must have been corrupted by him.

In his letters, Francis painted himself as not only hero but martyr. He had tried to do his duty and had nearly been killed for it, but he bore no malice. After the duel he hoped his friends would drop all personal hostility to Hastings. 'Let him be condemned or acquitted by the evidence that exists of his whole conduct. As I lay bleeding on the ground and when I thought the wound was mortal, I gave him my hand in token of forgiveness. From that moment to the end of my life, I am neither his friend or his foe.' It was all very noble.

As for the evidence Francis believed would convict Hastings, he spent his last few months in India collecting as much as he could. He already had a great deal, on the Rohilla war, on the judicial murder of Nand Kumar, on bribes, on the Maratha war. And now, as he was preparing to leave, he was presented with something that was so potentially powerful a charge that it would not only blow up Hastings but the Chief Justice, Sir Elijah Impey, as well. This added an extra satisfaction for Francis, for his dislike, his hatred, of Impey was only slightly less than his hatred of Hastings.

Francis's attitude to Impey had always been conditioned by the latter's friendship for the governor-general, but Francis also disliked the Supreme Court itself as an institution, a dangerous institution, interfering in the lives and actions of the British in Bengal. To these motives had been added a more personal animus. It had all come about because of the charms of seventeen-year old Mrs Grand, whose amorous exploits finally led to marriage with Napoleon's foreign minister, Talleyrand. Carefully selecting an evening when he knew Mrs Grand would be dining with Barwell, Francis, wearing a dark suit, scaled the wall of Grand's house with the aid of a bamboo ladder and made for Mrs Grand's bedroom. When her maid discovered the door locked, she roused the menservants. Trying to leave discreetly, Francis was caught, a bribe was refused. Calling for help from three of his friends who had accompanied him as far as the garden Francis managed to escape but one of them was captured and held to await Mr Grand, called hurriedly from his dinner. The next day Grand challenged Francis to a duel which Francis declined; it was, he said, 'a complete mistake'. Grand then sued Francis in the Supreme Court for damages of £160,000. The case took some months and to Francis's embarrassment ended with judgement against him for £5,000. He blamed the decision on the Chief Justice.

There was very little that Francis could do about the case. He might have taken an appeal to England, but that would only have caused him scandal, as he had left his wife behind there. But Impey, and Hastings, put a possible weapon into his hands. In doing so Hastings had once again been thinking of the interests of British India and not his own, or indeed any individual's. At the time his overriding concern was with the impending crises in the west and the south. His actions were entirely pragmatic with no real thought for the long-term consequences.

Despite Hastings's personal relationship with Impey, the Supreme Court's role as an institutional part of British administration was the cause of continuing friction between the Court and the executive. That friction was often muted but occasionally produced a flame, usually caused by some of the judges insisting on the very widest interpretation of the Court's powers, particularly concerning Indians, and on revenue matters. Though Council had restrained the judges from establishing jurisdiction over all Bengal, the vagueness of the Act which had established the Court left plenty of opportunity for the revival of controversy. In September 1780, Hastings came up with a solution which he believed would remove the essential conflict between the Court and the Council. It was to amalgamate the two systems of the Company's courts and the Supreme Court by making the chief justice the chief judge of the Company's Court of Appeal. This Court had hitherto consisted of the Governor-General-in-Council. It was a solution which would not only smooth relations between the two legal systems but remove from the executive a burden of legal work for which its members were not really qualified.

When the suggestion was put to members of Council on 3 October Francis and Wheler opposed it and the resolution was only passed with the help of Coote and the governor-general's casting vote. Impey accepted the post, which could be revoked by Council. He also accepted the salary that went with it. Francis was delighted. The whole affair was of very doubtful legality and the Regulating Act could be construed as being actually hostile. However, there was no doubt that Impey's acceptance of a second salary could easily be shown as corrupting the independence of the chief justice of the Supreme Court. The Court had been established to stand above the corruption of the executive government and to police its members. Now the chief justice had accepted an office under that government and the salary that went with it.

To the last moment Francis remained his old self, vehement in opposition and uncompromising even at the time of worst peril. He would not support Hastings's actions for the relief of Madras or any measures that seemed to suit the crisis. He seems on one occasion almost to have decided not to go, but he no longer had allies in Council. Taking his profits, variously estimated as being between £50,000 and £160,000, Philip Francis sailed for England on 2 December 1780.

There were many to congratulate Hastings on the departure of his enemy, an enemy who would have pulled down the frail structure of British India, just in the hope that it would bury the man he so hated. Francis left behind a legacy, a government with a 'war either actual or depending in every quarter', enfeebled by years of in-fighting and intrigue. Hastings hoped that with Francis gone there would be freedom to act decisively and without constantly looking over his shoulder for the stab in the back. 'I have power,' he wrote, 'and I will employ it.'

Back in London the Opposition in Parliament took up the 'Indian question' as a bundle of rods with which to chastise the government. One such rod was Muhammed Ali, nawab of Arcot, who had once been nawab of the Carnatic by courtesy of the British. They had made him ruler and they had made him pay for it – so much so, in fact, that he had been forced to borrow money from private individuals. Hastings had thought it 'infamous to plunder a plundered man'. It was, of course, in the interests of the nawab's creditors to encourage him to any sort of activity that might result in profit for them. Out of this welter of self-interest there came into existence a most powerful political lobby – in London. Unfortunately for Hastings his agent Lachlan Macleane was also agent for the nawab!

The Opposition in Parliament chose for their own purposes to create a myth. It was to the effect that the nawab of Arcot exercised some sinister influence over the government. The rumour was put about that the nawab's agent had bought control of seven or eight seats in the House of Commons and through bribery was able to influence government policy. At this time the nawab was actually so poor that he was unable to pay his own agent, let alone bribe members of the British parliament! In fact, it was not the impecunious nawab that anybody had to fear, but his creditors, violent men who would stop at little to protect their own capital and interest. Indeed, in 1776, they went so far as to arrest the governor of Madras, Lord Pigot, and imprison him. In the following year he died, while still under restraint.

It was an easy matter to smear Hastings by his association with the nawab's agent, Macleane. In 1777, an Opposition member claimed that the nawab of Arcot 'had an ambassador here . . . a Mr Macleane who he heard, as soon as he effected the nawab's business by the destruction of Lord Pigot, was to return back as ambassador from the King of Great Britain to the nawab. It seemed likewise that he had a third master, Mr Hastings . . . that Mr Hastings had recommended Mr Macleane to the nawab; and it might be fairly concluded from all this, that his Highness and Mr Hastings were the contrivers of the arrest and imprisonment of Lord Pigot'. But for all this menacing rubbish in London, it was to be Madras and the British there that were to present Hastings with his next threat.

In June 1780 Haidar Ali, the ruler of Mysore, 'resolved in the gloomy recesses of a mind capacious of such things, to leave the whole Carnatic an everlasting monument of vengeance . . . A storm of universal fire blasted every field, consumed every house, destroyed every temple . . . those who were able to avoid this tempest fled to the walled cities; but escaping from fire and sword and exile, they fell into the jaws of famine'. The purple prose of Edmund Burke hardly over-colours the reality, though the storm was very selective in where it hit, and even Burke had difficulty in describing its effect on the British in Madras. In fact they did nothing until the fires of burning villages could be clearly seen and the enemy was at the gates of the city. Panic moved among the British, heightening incompetence and even shattering men of worth. The commander-in-chief, Sir Hector Munro, victor of the battle of Buxar which firmly established British dominion in Bengal, listened to the sound of gunfire a few miles away when a force under Colonel Baillie was being annihilated – and did nothing except retreat in disorder, losing his guns and stores. When Hastings heard firm news late in September, it was of a Madras cut off from the hinterland that supplied its food and surrounded on all sides but the sea by Haidar's troops. The prestige which had been restored by Goddard and Popham in the west melted away in the flames of burning villages in the south.

The situation could hardly have been more menacing. Francis at least was going, but in Eyre Coote, Hastings had a commander-in-chief with no faith in final victory. The treasury was almost empty, and there was news of a French fleet of seven ships of the line with 7,000 troops on board, on its way to the Coromandel coast. And in Haidar, a soldier of genius, there was an enemy, subtle, energetic, determined. It was a state of affairs for which, ironically, Hastings's struggle with Francis and his assorted enemies at home had prepared him. Hastings had been compelled to turn to his inner resources, not only for defence against intrigue and innuendo, but to keep the administration of British India going at all. He too had become subtle, a fighter who used any means at his disposal. In one sense this limited his vision, for the years of struggle had eroded his trust in other men, and in their ideas. Self-reliance often stimulates suspicion and insensitivity: it did so in Hastings. But it also produced a ruthlessness of purpose and nothing was more necessary if anything was to be retrieved from the débâcle in the south.

Within two days of hearing the terrible news from Madras, Hastings had decided his policy. On 25 September he informed the Council what he proposed to do. He had already placed a ban on the movement of shipping from Calcutta and transferred as much bullion as he could reasonably allow from the depleted funds at his disposal. He opened simply. 'This is not,' he said, 'a time either for long deliberation . . . or the formal and tedious process of negotiation.' On the contrary, what was needed were 'the most instant, powerful and even hazardous exertions'. Men and money must be sent to Madras. With them there must be a new commander, for Haidar had demoralized those already there. Eyre Coote must go, for with his experience, the appeal of his reputation, so much of it acquired in the south, he was 'the only instrument to retrieve our past disgraces'. As for the Marathas, they must be neutralized by a negotiated peace.

Francis and Wheler were against him, maintaining that the south was lost and that Bengal must be defended until help could arrive from England. But such help was unlikely to be much. The war with the American colonies marched on into disaster, while the rebels were supported first by France and then by Spain, widening the war to Europe and the East. But Hastings would not have defeatism. 'While I have a soldier, or a rupee, I will never abandon the Carnatic; for if we do not fight Haidar Ali on that country, we shall have to fight him here.' With Coote's support and his own casting vote, Hastings's policies were put into effect.

At the end of October, Coote sailed with his troops. His orders were straightforward and precise. First he was to remove Governor Whitehill whose senseless provocation had brought Haidar down on Madras. Coote was then to do everything he could to defeat Haidar. Coote did his best but it was to be some time before he could produce a consequential victory while other commanders continued to suffer defeats. The fifth column among the Company's servants in Madras resisted Hastings's policies with every means they could find. When the nabob Muhammed Ali suggested that all the revenues of the Carnatic should be given to the Company, Hastings accepted, though safeguarding the nawab's interests. It was the best way of keeping the hands of the nawab's creditors off the revenues when those revenues were most needed. The complaints of the creditors would one day be embodied in Hastings's impeachment, but at least the directors gave him their support. Hastings was considerably helped by the arrival in June of a new Governor of Madras, Lord Macartney, a man of very different character to that of his predecessors.

Coote was constantly criticizing the governor-general and had to be calmed. Hastings was convinced that Coote was needed in Madras. In spite of his pessimism, he was still the best soldier the

British had. With infinite patience, Hastings soothed the old general, mediated between him and Macartney when his prickliness had drawn blood, defended him against the recriminations of the Madras Council. No matter was too small to attract the governor-general's concern, no gesture too insignificant to be made if it contributed to the running of the war. Hastings was a war-leader of Churchillian stature – and failings – but a war-leader without facility of communication, cut off by the vast spaces of India from his generals and diplomats. In May 1781, Hastings made preparations to draw in some of the long threads and make a journey himself to northern India.

There were matters, Hastings believed, that demanded his personal attention. There was the perennial problem of Mughal Delhi which could either be incited against Sindia or left for him to conquer. That depended on whether there was any real possibility of an alliance between Sindia and the British. There was the nawab of Oudh moving, it seemed, further and further into financial anarchy. And Chait Singh of Banaras, once again refusing to pay the tribute demanded of him. Then, there must be a meeting with the chief minister of the raja of Berar, which could produce 'a new political system, and decide the future fortune of the British interest in India'. The rains were coming and during the wet season military operations would be virtually suspended. There was even harmony in Council, for Hastings now had Wheler's confidence. Granted by Council full diplomatic powers and the command of all the Company's forces in the north. Hastings left Calcutta on 7 July 1781.

He took a large staff but only a small escort. For all the diplomatic potentialities of the journey one factor weighed perhaps more heavily than the others, and that was the necessity of raising money to pay for the war against Haidar. Hastings did not foresee personal danger, which was why he had kept the escort down to only two companies of soldiers. Mrs Hastings and two other ladies were with the governor-general's party and it was expected that the chief justice and his wife would join them at Banaras or Patna. The painter, William Hodges, went along to capture picturesque views for the delight of Europe.

The party moved slowly, staying for a few days at Murshidabad, the old capital of Bengal, where Hastings gave the young nawab fatherly advice. At Monghyr Hastings decided to leave Mrs Hastings and travel somewhat faster to Patna and then to Buxar on the frontier of the Company's territory. There on 12 August he was met by Chait Singh. The raja appeared with offensive ostentation, surrounded by 2,000 men and filling the river with his boats. Though Hastings received him, it was frigidly, refusing to accept the customary offer of the raja's turban as a token of his inferior position. Nor would Hastings discuss business. That must be done at Banaras where Hastings had decided to demand 5 million rupees, the equivalent in the terms of the times of half a million pounds sterling.

Hastings's treatment of Chait Singh was to form one of the main indictments against him. The raja's legal position was quite clear. The majority under Francis in the Council had made him in 1775 a 'tributary landlord', his position entirely dependent on the prompt and full payment of tribute, the revenues of the territory, which belonged to the Company. He had, however, been allowed his own coinage and his own police. Whatever his legal position, and Hastings was to give various and conflicting versions of what he as governor-general understood it to be, when money was required, Chait Singh was squeezed. When war with France had broken out, Chait Singh was asked to contribute half a million rupees to equip three battalions of infantry. In 1779, the same demand was made and Hastings used his casting vote to overrule the objections of Francis and Wheler. It was a matter, he said, of 'extraordinary emergencies' outweighing the raja's legal obligations. The following year when another demand was due. Chait Singh offered 200,000 rupees to Hastings as a bribe. This was accepted, but not as a bribe, and used by Hastings for purposes of state.

All these demands Chait Singh tried to resist, by delay and

with pleas that he had insufficient funds. Yet this 'tributary landlord' kept a personal force of 30,000 men, and his forts, it was said, were stocked with French weapons and ammunition. His territory was tattered by 'murder, robbery and rapine'. The man appointed by the British to look after Chait Singh's affairs was said to be his mother's lover and possibly his father. Above all, Chait Singh had tried to intrigue with Hastings' enemies in Council and there seems little doubt that he was happy to spread around details of Haidar Ali's successes in the south. In April 1781 it was reported to Hastings that 'if any serious accidents happen to our arms, he [Chait Singh] has told his minions he will declare independence'. The evidence against Chait Singh is all from British sources or from men beholden to them, but it cannot be dismissed because of that. It would be surprising if any man in Chait Singh's position had not tried to resist what were undoubtedly illegal demands made upon him, though in India at the time the only genuine legality was the power to enforce such demands.

Hastings's attitude to Chait Singh was Indian rather than British. In fact, in thirty years of immersion in India, he had absorbed the country's political morality. The justification was clear. The Company's dominion in India was not that of a European state either actual or ideal. The Company was an Indian power for all its European overtones. Indian rulers considered it as such and expected it to act as if it was. Hastings might be condemned for behaving like the worst of Indian rulers, but his reasons were absolutely valid in Indian terms. The Company's state was threatened with extinction and must defend itself with every means at its disposal.

Chait Singh was not to be alone in his suffering. The surviving Rohilla leader, Faizullah Khan, was ordered to supply a contingent of cavalry which he had agreed to produce for the nawab of Oudh in an emergency, and Hastings was determined that Oudh should find somewhere the one and a half million pounds that it was now in arrears to the Company.

127

Hastings made the elementary mistake of misjudging both Chait Singh and neglecting the fundamentals of Indian policy – he thought he could discipline a feudatory without the aid of military power. In doing so he sparked a rebellion that might have destroyed him, and the Company's state.

Arriving in Banaras, its narrow streets crowded with armed men and the pilgrims who came to visit, and to die in, this most sacred of Hindu holy places, Hastings had no apprehension of danger. He settled into a country house on the outskirts of the city and next morning sent Chait Singh a statement of his offences, demanding an immediate explanation of his behaviour. The answer, when it came that evening, was judged by Hastings to be a collection of 'shuffling excuses and palpable falsehoods'. His agent, Markham, who carried the messages did not agree that the raja's answer was provocative. But Hastings would have none of it. At ten in the evening Hastings ordered Markham to arrest Chait Singh.

Early next day, 16 August, this was done. Two companies of sepoys were sent to guard the raja in his own palace. Hastings took no immediate further action, as his Persian interpreter could not be found. In any case, it was time for the midday meal, and he did not wish to eat alone, so Markham could not be spared. This was a mistake. Chait Singh had lost face, that fragile though necessary shelter for superiority. At midday Markham received a note from one of the subalterns of the guard, telling him that boatloads of armed men could be seen crossing the river. Compounding drama with farce, the note informed Markham that for some reason the sepoys of the guard had not been issued with ammunition. Even with their useless muskets the guard had made no attempt to restrict access to their prisoner. Before another company of sepoys carrying ammunition could go in aid of the guard, the palace had been surrounded by Chait Singh's men, the gates broken in and most of the guard massacred. Chait Singh, descending the walls down a rope of turbans, made first for a fortress across the river and then to

Peace treaty at Benares, Oudh 1774

European House, Chapra, circa 1796

Cartoon including the figures of Sheridan, Fox, Burke, Impey, Hastings and Thurlow

Cartoon 'The Nabob Rumbled'

The House of Commons in 1793 by K. A. Hickel

Sir Elijah Impey, by Zoffany 1783

Warren Hastings, by Romney 1795

Daylesford House

Daylesford House; Chimney Piece

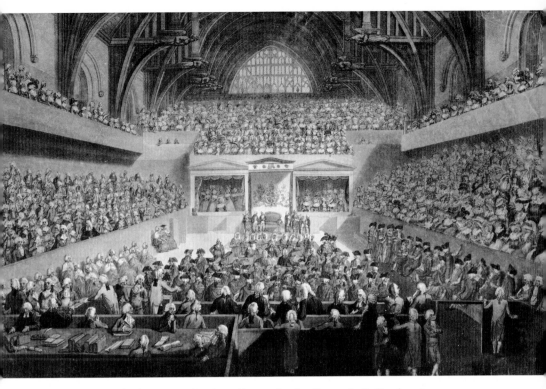

Trial of Warren Hastings. Engraving by Dayes & Pollard, 1789

Charles Cornwallis, by Gainsborough

another some ten miles away.

Chait Singh's escape, the massacre of soldiers both British and Indian, for the raja's men did not spare the British officers, who were not killed but mutilated, and within a few hours rebellion throughout the whole of the Banaras territory – was a disaster both personal and political. Hastings, in his letters to Wheler, radiated calm. His action, he told him, must have precipitated a long-planned rising: 'it was a mine sprung before its time'. It may well have been. Chait Singh appears to have been in contact with the enemies of the British. But it was just as likely that it was spontaneous anger at the way the raja had been treated. The cause hardly mattered at the time. Hastings had with him only four hundred men, all but thirty of whom were Indian soldiers. The nearest British troops were twenty miles away, and his position at Banaras was not defensible. There were several days before relief arrived, days in which the raja's men could be seen gathering on both sides of the river. Even when the British force arrived, an artillery officer disobeying orders got himself caught in the narrow alleys of the town and was killed with half his men. The rest of the force fell back on Chunar.

Hastings could not expect to hold his present position, nor did he wish to retreat. The governor-general taking to flight? It was unthinkable. But the governor-general dead would be worse. As Coote wrote to Wheler, 'Had an accident happened to Mr Hastings, what in the name of God could you or I have done with the government?' Even so, panic had spread to the British. At Patna where once Mir Kasim's men had massacred the British, memories flooded in, blocking judgement, and if it had not been for Mrs Hastings, who had moved up to the town from Monghyr, reminding them of their duty, the British would have fled and precipitated a rising. At Banaras, Hastings was cut off from everything but rumour. He accepted his officers' advice and left.

The little party made its way through the suburbs of Banaras in the darkest part of the night, the rain-wet trees and flowers filling the air with perfume. But there was also the smell of fear, as the servants and the baggage-carriers were on the edge of hysteria – justified, as it turned out, for, taking a different road, they were ambushed by Chait Singh's men. Accompanying Hastings was the diplomatic agent of the raja of Berer who refused to leave the governor-general though it meant leaving his own family in Banaras in possible danger. After a short march the party met up with the relief column from Chunar and returned with it to the safety of the fort there. At Chunar, Hastings learned that his wife had moved to Patna and was greatly concerned for her safety. He wanted her to return to Calcutta, but in the end agreed that she could remain at Bhagalpur, a hundred miles or so down-river from Patna.

At Chunar Hastings had to borrow clothes and money. The Berar agent offered him a loan, but the money was in Banaras and Hastings was not prepared to endanger the lives of the agent's family by having it sent from there. He could do little until reinforcements came. He would not accept aid from the nawab of Oudh and in skirmishes with Chait Singh's men it was the British who were coming off worse. He spent much time considering his own actions. Had he been responsible for the rising? Whatever happened he expected to be blamed for it, and began to prepare a defence.

Hastings did not allow himself to be diverted from wider matters, the terms to be offered Sindia in particular. But he was also quick to commend men who had not waited for orders but acted, like Colonel Morgan at Cawnpore, who had immediately marched to his relief. On 11 September the time had come to take the offensive against Chait Singh. Hastings decided not to attack the fortress of Banaras itself but those others held by Chait Singh and the bulk of his men, estimated at some 30,000 in all. Within ten days, the two principal fortresses had fallen and Chait Singh, leaving his mother in his last remaining stronghold, had fled with camel-loads of gold into the jungles of Bundelkhand.

'Our credit and influence are restored', Hastings wrote to

his wife, even before the raja had fled, and that sea-change which in India always followed a restatement of power was soon apparent. At Banaras on 28 September, Hastings enthroned a young boy as raja, with his father as his deputy. Control of the police he placed in the hands of a Muslim who had once been a servant to Mir Kasim. The raja now had no special privileges, but was just what Hastings had said his predecessor had been, a 'tributary landlord'. As a gesture, Hastings abolished the pilgrim tax in Banaras and reduced many of the custom tolls. As for Chait Singh's mother, still defending the fort at Bijaigurh, Hastings told Popham, now on his way to take it, that she must be treated with dignity. But Popham, disregarding his own promise to the rani that if she surrendered neither she nor members of her household would be searched, divided the property among his officers and men. A loosely worded letter from Hastings had given Popham a loophole. Hastings refused gifts of a jewelled sword and some fine boxes for Mrs Hastings. All he wanted, he said, was the manuscripts from Chait Singh's library.

In October, Hastings was joined by his wife and the Impeys in Banaras. He would stay for two months more in the hope of finalizing terms with Sindia who had agreed to preliminaries of peace. While at Chunar, Hastings had signed a new treaty with the nawab of Oudh, from which he had great expectations, though he had some doubts about how the terms would be received in Council. He had not consulted Wheler, Coote was far away, and the man appointed to take Barwell's place, John Macpherson, only reached Calcutta in October 1781. Hastings asked Macpherson to join him at Banaras. It was as if he had suddenly realized that he would need support. The Council had asked a number of questions, which seemed to him to be loaded with phrases such as 'if the governor-general had been even harsh and unjust'. Nor did Macpherson join him at Banaras.

Hastings was set to work perfecting a justification of all his actions, his *Narrative of the Insurrection*. The *Narrative* is not the plea of a guilty man but of one who had totally identified the interests of British India with himself. Fully polished, the *Narrative* was ready at the end of December to be sent off to Major Scott for publication in England. It is a remarkable document. In it, Hastings sees himself as 'the essence of the State itself', and 'talisman'. He may have lost Banaras with a revenue of 2 million rupees, but had regained it as one producing twice as much – out of apparent disaster had come 100 per cent profit! While everything was at its blackest in Banaras 'I continued a successful negotiation of peace' with Sindia. And he had demonstrated the power of British India in such a way that it would enhance 'the permanency of British influence' with more effect than 'the most splendid victories'.

There is more in the *Narrative* than a justification for events in Banaras. A bright thread in the pattern is the problem of Oudh. And it was a problem that had the more unsavoury elements of an Indian Night's Entertainment. The country, once rich and prosperous, had been slowly ground into anarchy both political and financial. Banaras, one of its richest provinces, had been cut away and given to Chait Singh with the enormous quit-rent of constant demand by the Company. The Clavering–Francis coalition had imposed an even larger subsidy on the nawab and demanded ever more money for the support of what was still known as a 'temporary' brigade of Company troops. British officers commanded the nawab's army – a rabble which merely existed as a justification for corruption. The nawab, Asaf-ud-daulah, had, hardly surprisingly, 'abandoned himself to dissipation', though he spent much of the money he had – or at least his credit – on the collecting of clocks and watches.

The nawab, like some eastern Prometheus, had feeding on his vitals European vultures, disguised as the Company's agents, who 'robbed him without scruple, by loans advanced at an exorbitant interest and pensions wrung from him in return'. Colonel Hannay, who had been appointed in 1778 to collect the revenue from three districts, departed after three years with

£300,000. When it was later suggested that he might return, the nawab wrote to Hastings: 'Colonel Hannay is inclined to request your permission to be employed in the affairs of this quarter. If, by any means, any matter of this country dependent on me should be entrusted to the Colonel, I would not remain here, but will go from hence to you'.

The nawab's enemies were not only the British: there were his grandmother and his mother, the 'Begums' as they were known. His mother hated the nawab and still deeply resented the settlement the British had forced her to make with her son. He responded with constant quarrelling, and it was only the British guarantees to the two Begums that prevented the nawab from expropriating their property for his own use. Hastings himself had officially stated 'that our faith and credit must prevent . . . even the appearance of oppression on a person of the Begum's rank, character and sex'. Francis had not accepted this, as he believed, quite rightly, that the Begums had inherited their fortune in direct violation of Muslim law and precedent. Perhaps the reason Hastings had originally defended the Begums' case was that Francis opposed it!

Times, however, had changed. Francis was in England, the security of British dominion in India was in peril. The Begums had money – and there was 'proof' of their conspiracy against the British. Most of it came from Colonel Hannay. His revenue-collecting methods inspired opposition and this he interpreted as support for Chait Singh. There is evidence that the Begums permitted agents of the 'raja' to recruit from among their dependants, and that there was considerable civil disorder on their estates, though this, in fact, had died down before the end of 1781.

The treaty which Hastings had signed with the nawab at Chunar in September 1781 had, in fact, been full of concessions. The 'temporary' brigade was abolished and the nawab would no longer have to support Colonel Hannay and his men. The nawab would be allowed to take back the estate of the Rohilla Faizullah

Khan in return for a cash allowance and any other such estates. This could be taken to apply to those held by the two Begums. Hastings's excuse for this clause was that 'the nawab demanded it, and with what face could I refuse it?' But a few days later, Hastings disclosed to his agent, Middleton, at the nawab's capital of Lucknow, that the whole – even the sole – purpose of the treaty was to ensure the payment of the outstanding sums owed to the British. The reduction in the nawab's costs and the seizure of various estates would bring in money immediately.

The actual situation in Oudh was no secret to Hastings. 'Lucknow,' he wrote to Macpherson, 'was a sink of iniquity. It was the school for rapacity.' And he was referring to the behaviour of the British who had taken advantage of the relations between the nawab and the Company to enter his service and profit from it. 'What will you say,' Hastings went on, 'of beardless boys rejecting with indignation gratuities of 3,000 and 5,000 rupees? What will you think of clerks in office clamouring for principalities, threatening those who hesitated to gratify their wants with the vengeance of patronage . . . and what of a city with as many independent and absolute sovereignties as there are Englishmen in it?' There is proof of Hastings's awareness of the evil, and yet his action against the Begums seems only part of it.

His justification was that the Begums, particularly the younger one, had supported Chait Singh. She 'by her own conduct, and that of all her agents and dependants during the Banaras trouble, had forfeited every claim she had to the protection of the English Government'. Her sole aim had been the 'general extirpation' of the British 'race and power in Hindustan'. Whatever Hastings said then and later in his defence, this was the gravamen of his charge and the stated motive for his actions. As such it had the support of the terror of the times. Yet the nawab was reluctant to move against his own family, even though Hastings had made it quite clear that it was he who must act. A variety of pressures was put upon him, including a visit by Impey who informed Middleton after his return to Banaras that Hastings was most pleased with the way things were going and added, 'I need not mention the necessity of taking care that the money be applied to the Company's use'. In fact the whole campaign against the Begums was no more than a device to produce sufficient money to pay the nawab's debts to the British.

In December 1781, Hastings's letters to Middleton were heavy with menace. What was Middleton doing about the matter of the Begums? Their wealth must be confiscated, and quickly. There must also be some Englishman present when the nawab finally took action to see that he did not go too far but also to ensure that he did not weaken, for the Begums must be put 'at the entire mercy of the nawab'. If Middleton was not capable of carrying out these instructions he must say so and the governor-general would come to Lucknow himself.

Threats of one sort or another at last produced action, and the nawab finally marched against the Begums in their palace at Faizabad, the old capital of Oudh, in January 1782. At this time, Hastings was travelling down-river to Calcutta, but he was still prepared to threaten the nawab with his own presence if he procrastinated and Middleton with unstated reprisals if he did not get on with finding the Begums' treasure. At last on 25 January, Middleton was able to report that 'after using some severities' with the eunuchs who managed the Begums' household, 'we at length came at the secret hoards'. Some 5 million rupees were initially found but there was believed to be more. The eunuchs were placed in irons and threatened with torture, though when it was applied it seems to have been mild, for it took nearly a year for the prisoners to break down.

Hastings was incensed by the slowness with which the money was produced, yet the first amount of 5 million rupees went straight into the Company's account. He censured Middleton for inactivity and would not allow him to resign until all the nawab's debts had been paid in full. He then recalled Middleton and replaced him with Bristow, the man he had removed for corruption. Hastings's actions were once again edged with the psychotic, wild and reckless, empty of sound judgement. Hastings had sent back home the justificatory *Narrative* which he said was written so that 'every intelligent old woman in England' could understand. But he was mistaken. The 'old women' of the Houses of Parliament refused to understand and in October 1782 Hastings learned that the Commons had passed resolutions to recall both him and Impey.

But before this news arrived to subvert Hastings's authority and prestige once again, there were wars to be settled and the peace to be won. By the time Hastings returned to Calcutta after six months absence, Sindia had been detached from the coalition against the British and was helping to mediate between them and the other Maratha leaders. Hastings was in a great hurry to settle the Maratha problem. The real danger he saw as being in the south where Coote had still been unable to produce a major victory. To his agent, endlessly talking at Poona, Hastings insisted that 'it is not peace with conditions of advantage that we want, but a speedy peace; and we would rather purchase it with the sacrifice of every foot of ground that we have acquired from the Marathas, excepting Salsette and the little islands adjacent to Bombay, than hazard the loss of the present opportunity by contending for more . . .'

Yet matters moved slowly until finally a treaty was signed at Salibhai in May 1782. All the territories the British had taken from the Peshwa were to be restored, all Europeans except British and Portuguese were to be excluded from the Maratha dominions – it was hoped by this to get rid of the French mercenaries with the Maratha armies and thus eliminate French influence. Haidar Ali was mentioned in the treaty as being obliged by it to restore territory he had seized, and the Maratha leaders agreed to bring pressure upon him. It was a forlorn hope, and when Haidar was informed of the terms of the treaty by an envoy from Coote, he said he had never heard of it, which was true, and that he had no intention of ending hostilities. If Coote thought the Marathas would be of help to him, he was mistaken: 'Bring the Nizam and the Marathas to help you, and see what you can do. You were all three united for a time once before, and what did it end in? And what think you will it come to in the future? Why, each will go back the same way he came'. Haidar had replied to a message from Sindia asking him what his intentions were, quite simply, 'I am bent upon war.'

All was not particularly well with the Maratha treaty either, as the Peshwa was prevaricating over ratification. In fact he was waiting to see whether Haidar Ali would inflict a crushing defeat on the British. Coote had managed to produce something of a stalemate but no more – though this was an achievement as he was short of supplies and men, and weighed down by his own pessimism. There was a steady stream of complaints to Hastings, most of them unjustified but not easily soothed. Coote, too, was tired and ill, yet oddly full of courage. Whatever his personal feelings, he pressed on, winning a major victory at Porto Novo in July 1781. But it was an isolated defeat for Haidar, who avoided set-piece battles. He was a guerrilla genius operating in a land scorched with fire and whitened by the bones of the dead. Cattle were stolen by Haidar's men almost under the eyes of the British troops and the land could not be worked by the peasants in safety. 'A day's rice,' Coote wrote in one despatch, 'may decide the fate of the British Empire in India'. After a year of this, Hastings saw nothing, no decisive advantages gained, 'and we lose men by every victory'.

In February 1782 a French fleet under Admiral Suffren fought a drawn battle off Madras with British ships, but in April was able to land nearly 3,000 men and guns at Pondicherry. After three more engagements Suffren captured the British admiral's base in Ceylon. Against bitter protests from Madras, the admiral then sailed away to Bombay to refit, not to return until April 1783. But late in 1782 some changes for the better in the prosecution of the war were taking place. Coote, instead of dashing about the country trying vainly to bring Haidar to battle, was at last persuaded by Hastings to stand on the defensive. This and the death of Haidar early in December appeared at last to be giving the British some advantage. Haidar's death inspired the Peshwa to ratify the treaty of Salibhai. Regrettably, it did not end the war in the south.

In part this was due to the determination of Haidar's son, Tipu, to continue the fight, but perhaps more so to the inability of the British in Madras to take advantage of their enemy's death. Despite Hastings's ruthless attempt to control the Madras Council and the multifarious interests which bedevilled it, Madras remained an anarchy of indecision, private interest and active sedition. In one sense it was lack of discipline, the refusal to take orders, especially from a governor-general many hundreds of miles away. Soldiers acted on their own instincts without thought for any larger issues and frequently refused orders from the civilian authorities. Essentially it was a conflict of personalities. At the centre of this conflict was the governor of Madras, George Macartney.

For India, his personality was unusual. He was not a Company man nor had he ever been in India before his appointment in Madras. He had had wide political experience in Europe, including a diplomatic mission to Catherine the Great of Russia, had been chief secretary in Ireland, and was a member of the English political establishment by marriage and by acquaintance in the highest places. There is little wonder that Macartney found British India provincial and petty, and it was just as natural that he misunderstood Indian politics. He was convinced that the real enemies were not the Indian states, but Holland and France. Barely a month after his arrival in June 1781, Macartney proposed peace to Haidar. He was quite sure that the war in the south had been a direct consequence of the war with the Marathas and he blamed Hastings for that. Macartney's first official response to Hastings's letters was reasonably conciliatory, as was that of the governor-general to him. But it soon became clear that Macartney was not prepared to take orders from Hastings. Not only that, but he began to lecture Hastings, and not only about future policy but about that of the past. In the case of the revenues taken over by Hastings from the nawab of Arcot before Macartney's arrival, the new governor went much further than had been contemplated by Hastings and took over the nawab's sovereign rights himself! At first Hastings was disposed to leave things as they were. But the intrigues of the nawab's English creditors undermined the governor's plans, and his own views on policy and responsibility steadily eroded the patience of Hastings.

The clash came when Hastings tried to mediate between the governor and Coote. Hastings had given Coote supreme command and maximum discretion – the pressure of the times demanded it. To all functional intent, the Madras government was in suspense. Macartney's arrival made no fundamental difference. The war in the south was being paid for from the revenues of Bengal and Hastings regarded it 'as our own'. Bluntly Macartney was told that he had no authority over the war, but the new governor could not agree. Unfortunately, embedded in the ambiguities of the Regulating Act was his justification. Conciliatory letters from Calcutta had no effect. Macartney stated, at considerable and tedious length, that the power given to Coote was illegal and that Hastings's argument in favour of it was 'so extraordinary and inadmissible that we can scarcely give credit to those senses which inform us that it proceeds from your Council'. Macartney even implied that Coote had been sent to Madras only to keep him away from his seat on the Bengal Council.

Coote played into Macartney's hands by allowing himself to give consideration to a suggestion by the nawab of Arcot that he accept the administration of his government. Coote was forbidden to do so by Hastings as soon as he heard of the proposal, but it added cement to Macartney's structure of complaint. The governor, too, was sending his own version of events back to London. Even when Coote, worn out, returned to Bengal in December 1782 to recuperate, the tensions and the misjudgements and foolish actions which emerged from them, remained. Hastings's weapons had always been words and he used them to the full. 'We look,' he wrote, 'to the arrival of every post from Madras – we open our letter and peruse its contents we may say, indeed, with astonishment.' Macartney's action was a breach of the treaty with the nawab. In fact, Hastings was determined that when Coote had recovered he would return to Madras with full authority to supersede Macartney should the governor continue in his attitude of defiance.

Until Coote left Bengal in March 1783, Macartney was constantly lashed by Hastings's comments and instructions. He must not negotiate with Haidar's son, Tipu. 'Nothing,' Hastings wrote, 'could be more fortunate than that you were not possessed of those powers of negotiation', for if he had been he would have rendered useless all Hastings's action in defence of the British presence in India. But when Coote actually left Calcutta Hastings did not give him the power to suspend Macartney. Council had not been prepared to endorse such authority – perhaps because of reports from London that the House of Commons had demanded Hastings's recall, though in fact these demands had been rejected by the Court of Directors. Perhaps it was the directors' own despatches criticizing Hastings's treatment of Chait Singh, which arrived in February 1783.

While Coote was away from Madras no attempt was made to capitalize on the death of Haidar. Coote's successor, General Stuart, who had been involved in the imprisonment of Lord Pigot, quarrelled with Macartney and was without military competence. At the time of Haidar's death, a move against his capital might well have ended the war in the enemy's confusion. But nothing was done, except that Macartney sent overtures of peace to Tipu which almost amounted to surrender. Fortunately for Hastings, Tipu was not interested in peace, but in victory, and rejected the proposals.

When Coote landed at Madras once again in April 1783, it was as a dying man. He had responded to the call of duty with his old courage but with the certainty that he 'had one foot in the grave and the other at the edge of it'. When nearing Madras he had been pursued by French warships and, in the excitement of the chase, had been struck 'with a paralytic stroke'. They had managed to escape the French but Coote had been unable to escape death. It meant that Macartney was free to do what he liked, subject of course, to the incompetence of his military commanders. One was caught in a trap by Tipu and soundly defeated. More importantly, the French were contributing to the scene not only with military action but in keeping alive Tipu's hopes of ultimate success.

What saved the British presence in the south from the incompetence of the military and the intransigence of Macartney was the fortunate arrival from Europe of the news that peace with France had been concluded. It came on 23 June, just in time to save Stuart from disaster. The French withdrew their troops. But it was to be almost another year before peace was concluded with Tipu.

While Hastings was fighting his wars in India and struggling against a multitude of enemies both British and Indian, that other war, for the reputation and future of Hastings himself, was still going on in England. There had been periods of quiet when old supporters like Lawrence Sulivan were back in places of power in the Company, but they did not last for long. In the Parliament elected in 1780, Hastings had only two allies, Sir Robert Palk and Francis Sykes, while those who had once supported Clive and Francis formed quite a considerable bloc. In a by-election the following year, Sir Thomas Rumbold increased the number of Hastings's enemies in the House of Commons, though Barwell also obtained a seat. Barwell did not like what he saw and heard in Parliament. It was a dangerous place; compared with Europe, he wrote to Hastings, 'India is innocence, the purest innocence'.

141

And yet Hastings's position did not seem threatened either by the government or by the directors. In the cabinet he had two firm supporters in Thurlow and Stormont. Even the prime minister, Lord North, seemed friendly, as the appointment of Macpherson to the Bengal Council, and later, of John Stables, a strong Hastings supporter, seemed to indicate. Sulivan was once again chairman of the Company. But Hastings's position was founded upon sand, and already his enemies were assembling for the first undermining. Burke and Fox were back in the new Parliament stronger than before. On the Opposition benches sat the younger William Pitt and Richard Brinsley Sheridan, the playwright and manager of Drury Lane Theatre. In April 1781 the Commons appointed a Secret Committee to investigate the causes of the war in the Carnatic and a Select Committee to enquire into the administration of justice in Bengal. The campaign against Hastings, which was not to end until fourteen years had passed, had opened.

Philip Francis arrived in England in October 1781, after an extremely long journey which he had used to compile a memorial to the directors, containing all his attacks on Hastings and his policies. Francis was well received at court, partly because he was believed to be a potential danger to the king and his supporters. But the directors ignored him until he forced a meeting with Sulivan which was followed by the formal acceptance by the directors of his memorial. In Parliament Francis turned to the Opposition. Edmund Burke was already an ally and used Francis in the Select Committee. Witnesses were coached by him, and those who were known to be supporters of Hastings were cruelly questioned, using material supplied by Francis. Nor was the Committee investigating the Carnatic war neglected. Francis produced a long series of questions, all of them strongly biased against Hastings. The chairman of the Committee was Henry Dundas, a Scot who believed that he had not been adequately rewarded by North for bringing a large number of Scottish seats to his support. Dundas was against the

American war. Seeing a great future for William Pitt he intended to be a part of it.

In November 1781 the news of the British defeat at Yorktown, the last great battle in the American war, arrived to shatter Lord North's government. In defence, the Prime Minister pointed to India and to Hastings as the saviour of the British presence there. Undaunted, Francis continued with his work of denigration, feeding material to both Burke and Dundas, organizing a war of pamphlets, some written by himself. He also managed to get the case of Nand Kumar on the agenda of the Select Committee. Nand Kumar, Francis exclaimed, 'is returned and like Caesar's ghost . . . is now raging for revenge'. When Major Scott, Hastings's agent, arrived in December he tried to answer Francis with other pamphlets but his talents were not up to it. The Francis version, full of apparently unassailable facts presented in the most sensational form, had sunk firmly into the minds of the interested public.

The first report of the Select Committee appeared in February 1782, and it was clear that the prejudice of its members had destroyed any sense of impartiality, and that only evidence unfavourable to Hastings had been heard. On 20 March an even more sinister and menacing event took place – the North ministry fell. Superficially, it seemed a triumph for the friends of Hastings, for two of his supporters took office; the Marquis of Rockingham and Lord Shelburne. But with Rockingham as prime minister, Edmund Burke had come to power. He was paymaster-general, his brother was secretary to the treasury. In April Edmund wrote to his cousin William, who was in Madras intriguing against Hastings, 'I think the reign of Sulivan is over, the reign of Hastings is over'. Indeed Burke controlled the fortunes of the new government. He threatened to resign and bring it down if the Indian problem was not investigated on lines laid down by himself. The support Rockingham and Shelburne had previously given to Hastings melted away: 'We entertain the highest personal regard for Mr Hastings but we cannot imperil the interests of the nation. We cannot to save an individual, however worthy, ruin our party and break up the government'.

Everything now seemed to move against Hastings. A new election of directors of the Company produced men hostile to the governor-general. The reports of the Committee were presented to the House of Commons and worked upon with all the embroidery of rhetoric. Though the House did not seem much interested in Burke's flood of abuse, resolutions were carried which ended with the demand that 'It was the duty of the Court of Directors to address the Crown for the recall of all those whom the House of Commons had censured'. When the news of the Banaras affair and the revolt of Chait Singh arrived, despite, or perhaps because of its inaccuracy, it was used to inflame opinion against Hastings and resulted in yet another resolution being carried in the House. This time it called specifically upon the directors to take steps to remove Hastings 'for having in sundry instances acted in a manner repugnant to the honour and policy of this nation'.

Hastings was saved by the action of the stockholders of the Company. Meeting together and with an overwhelming majority of 428 to 75, they voted that the 'Court of Directors were not bound to attend to any suggestions which emanate from any one branch of the legislature'. Burke and his friends were incensed and the morale of Hastings's friends revived. It was further raised by the death of Rockingham a few days later on 1 July, and the assumption of office by Lord Shelburne who was still, rather naively, thought to be a steadfast friend. But Shelburne was deserted by Burke and Fox and his position was tenuous to say the least. To consolidate his position, Shelburne needed the vital source of patronage that India provided. He first issued orders for the recall of Elijah Impey who had been severely censured by the Select Committee. He then sounded the directors about the recall of Hastings though, he insisted, with honour. The directors took the hint and began to criticize Hastings's actions in their despatches, ordering him to reinstate such men as

Bristow and condemning his arrest of Chait Singh as 'unwarrantable and highly impolitic'. Again the stockholders refused their support for Hastings's recall. When Parliament reassembled in December all factions seemed to be allied against Hastings, and Barwell wrote to him: 'Be prepared to quit your seat and the country at a moment's notice'.

The news of the Committee's resolutions reached India in October 1782 helping to undermine the governor-general's prestige at a time when such prestige was most in need of reinforcement. Hastings, however, would not be pushed into making a false peace with his Indian enemies. 'I wish,' he wrote, 'that our rulers would play at chess, and learn that even with the best play many pawns and capital pieces must be given and taken before the game can be won.' In February 1783 the directors' resolutions condemning his actions at Banaras arrived in Calcutta. 'Are they aware,' he wrote to Scott, 'that in their eagerness to vilify me, they sow the seeds of destruction and rebellion among their own subjects, and that a declaration so authentic in favour of a rebel' could destroy everything he was working for?

He sent off to Shelburne a carefully argued defence and warned him of the possible consequences that condemnation made public could have for the diplomatic moves in India that could lead to peace. To the directors, Hastings's defence was also an attack. For eleven years he had been governor-general, yet 'I have received nothing but reproach, hard epithets, and indignities instead of rewards and encouragement'. He claimed that he had really saved British India and told them that if they should insist on the reinstatement of Chait Singh he would immediately resign. By October 1783, Hastings had in fact made up his mind to go. Everyone, even those he had once thought of as his friends, seemed to have turned against him. Macpherson and Stables had virtually taken control of the Council with their influence over Wheler. Hastings had restored Bristow to the Residency at Lucknow on Macpherson's advice, and between the two of themthey were turning Oudh into an even worse state than before. But he would not leave immediately. Oudh must be settled. If only he could do that, 'I shall close my service with glory, and leave a lasting good name behind me'.

The problems of Oudh persuaded Hastings to ask permission of his Council to handle them personally at Lucknow. Permission given, he left Calcutta and arrived at Lucknow on 27 March 1784 and immediately set about devising reforms in the government. The ruler was weak and easily controlled but Hastings found him likeable and spent a great deal of time with him during his five months' stay. Basically the future of Oudh depended on whether there would be another failure of the rains. If there was, nothing could be done. Even the capital itself was 'a dreary picture of drought and infertility', with its dying and its dead in the streets. In July the rains fell heavily and continued for nearly three weeks, bringing the finest harvest for years. The rest was merely paper-work. Bristow's defalcations were referred to the Board of Revenue, cash payments and grants of food were made to the troops. New settlements of the land revenue were made. Better still, new officials were appointed and all of them Indians. 'I hope,' Hastings wrote to Council, 'that neither the present nor any future administration will think of committing the inferior detail to the control of a British subject. We have already too many English Collectors now in our own . . . districts. To establish them in this world would be to subvert the rights of the family, to injure the revenues, and to loosen the attachment of the peasants which it will be ever good policy to conciliate.' He believed that the steps he had taken would bring the country out of debt by the end of the year and into some sort of financial stability soon afterwards.

A visit to Banaras found the city prospering but the countryside devastated. Again changes were made in the administration which Hastings believed would bring on the necessary reforms. Most of Hastings's proposals were badly received by the members of Council in Calcutta, and there were

146

attempts to block some of his more essential measures. But the strongest clash came over Lord Macartney's attempts to bring peace to the south. From May onwards the conflicts intensified. Hastings had hoped to drive the new Mysore ruler, Tipu Sahib, to peace with the threat of a British–Maratha coalition. The treaty of Salibhai had been the first move in this strategy. But an instruction from the directors which was received late in 1783 demanded an immediate peace and Macartney set about getting one at almost, it seemed, any cost. Hastings had been compelled to agree to the attempt; he could hardly disobey the directors quite so flagrantly, but Macartney was warned to be very careful about terms. When the treaty was signed at Mangalore in March 1784, it turned out not only to be humiliating for the British but to contain no mention of that crucial figure, the nawab of Arcot, and to be offensive to the Marathas. The treaty was ratified by the Bengal Council without Hastings's prior approval, though the Council did instruct Macartney to insert a clause covering the nawab. Macartney ignored this, yet the Council also rejected Hastings's repeated advice that they should suspend Macartney. 'What a man is this Lord Macartney!' was Hastings's comment, 'The wit of man could not devise such effectual instruments of a nation's ruin as this black eagle portends to every land and state over which he casts the shadow of his wings. I yet believe that, in spite of peace, he will effect the loss of the Carnatic.'

Hastings also clashed with his Council over Delhi and the remnants of the Mughal empire which had been ravaged by war and rebellion. The emperor could not make up his mind which faction to support, potential claimants to his insecure throne were assassinated almost daily, and mutinous troops dominated the city. Hastings had an envoy in Delhi, Major James Browne, whose main task was to report on the ever-changing situation there. But Browne developed partisan emotions of his own. He was against Sindia and the Marathas and for an alliance with the Sikhs. He constantly advised the sending of British troops. A brigade was all that was needed to seize the city and the emperor and take control of affairs. Browne was not alone in his assumptions. When the governor-general reached Lucknow all the factions in the imperial capital were convinced that he was marching at the head of British troops on the city. Hastings denied this in a letter, but he was not believed and scepticism was confirmed, or so it seemed in Delhi, by the fact that in April 1784 the heir-apparent, Jahandar Shah, fled to Lucknow.

The arrival of Jahandar Shah demanded some sort of action on Hastings's part. The governor-general's first act was to assure the emperor that the heir-apparent had not come to Lucknow at *his* invitation. Meanwhile the emperor was assuring Browne that his son had not gone with his approval or consent. In fact, Jahandar Shah had fled to avoid the possibility of assassination. At the emperor's request, Browne left Delhi for Lucknow to discover the governor-general's intentions and to persuade him to send Jahandar Shah back to his father. Browne also carried a request for the renewed payment of the old Bengal tribute money so as to give the emperor 'some relief from his present emergent distresses'. At Lucknow, Browne learned that Jahandar Shah had been received by Hastings and the nawab with considerable pomp and display, all of which had been noted by spies for the information of their various masters at the courts of India. Hastings had been sympathetic to the prince and had seen him every day. He had been affected by his wretched condition; 'fallen as the House of Timur is, it is yet a relic of the most illustrious line of the Eastern world', as he wrote to the members of Council. He asked the artist Zoffany, who had accompanied him to Lucknow on the chance of commissions, to paint the prince's portrait. There remained the political consequences of the prince's flight. If he remained in Oudh he would become a centre of conflict and intrigue. Perhaps, Hastings suggested, he might be given refuge in the Company's territories? The Council would not agree and ordered Hastings to send the prince back to his father 'with safety and credit' and not to commit the Company to any specific course of action. It was a very wise embargo, as Hastings, 'ardently', as he wrote in a private letter to Wheler, wishing to 'close my service with some act that will reflect credit on my nation', was contemplating the possibility of putting Jahandar Shah on the Mughal throne! The heirs of the great Mughal emperors still represented a 'sovereignty univer- sally acknowledged though the substance of it no longer exists'. The mystique of a great empire operated the same powerful influence in India after its decline as the Roman empire had done in Europe. And those who sought dominion, whether Indian or European, also sought to profit from control over that influence.

Hastings was ahead of his time – and of the limitations of British power. The day would come when the British would be recognized as the successors to the Mughals, but it was as yet far away beyond the horizons of most men's minds.

In October 1784 Wheler died, leaving Hastings at the mercy of a hostile majority. The news from England which had followed him up-country had not been particularly encouraging either. William Pitt had won an election and his new India Bill contained just the sort of powers Hastings had been calling for. In his letters and conversation there was a slight weakening in his determination to go home. Scott had constantly told him that everyone in England would want him to stay, but 'why am I not told by authority?' As for Pitt, though he seemed to be a friend of the Company he had said nothing when Fox had attacked Hastings. If he was given a clear request to stay, he might think it his duty to do so, and yet with his wife now back in England and pregnant he would prefer to be at home. He could not make up his mind. At Calcutta he had an East Indiaman delayed for him and then changed his mind. He waited until the next year before, finally, deciding to go. On 7 February, Hastings left India for the last time. He could not have envisaged the extent of the ordeal that awaited him in England.

5

<h1 style="text-align:center">The Triumph of Probity
or
The Decline and Fall of the Nabob</h1>

<h3 style="text-align:center">[I] The Ordeal of Warren Hastings</h3>

13 February 1788. A cold, bright London day. Since before dawn there had been crowds on the approaches to Westminster Hall, where the High Court of Parliament was to sit in judgement. In its long history, this ancient building, nearly seven centuries old, had seen the acclamation of many kings, and one condemned to death, the trials of traitors and rebels. This time the accused was neither king, traitor nor rebel, but this hardly mattered to those who had come to watch. The mobs in the streets, bullied by cavalry into some sort of order behind lines of tall Grenadiers, would have to be content with rumour and the satirical broadsheets and vicious cartoons which had already prejudged the evidence. Those inside the Hall, the privileged, expected high drama.

Westminster Hall had certainly been prepared for the theatrical. Under the great window, looking down on an empty throne flanked by two royal boxes, were rows of seats for the ticket-holders, and more in galleries on either side of the long hall. Below, on the left of the throne, were rows of red-covered seats for members of the House of Lords, and opposite them, though this time covered in green, the places of members of the Commons. For the accused there was a little box near the door,

150

facing the throne and separated only by the witness-box from the seats of his accusers.

By ten o'clock most of the ticket-holders were in their seats; some – not there by right, it was said – had paid £50 for the privilege. The Queen and two of her daughters occupied the box of the Duke of Newcastle. There were a great many diamonds and feathers and not only on the ladies, for the ambassadors of the great kingdoms of Europe were treating this as a state occasion and were wearing their orders. In the audience were: that greatest of contemporary actresses, Sarah Siddons; the author of *The Decline and Fall of the Roman Empire*, Edward Gibbon, aware, no doubt, of being present at a crucial event in the rise of the British; and Joshua Reynolds, who had painted the accused's portrait just before he had left England almost twenty years ago.

By eleven o'clock the members of the Commons had taken their places, though significantly neither the prime minister nor any member of the Cabinet was present. As the clock struck the hour, the Lords entered the Hall. They were dressed in robes of ermine and gold. The heralds, under the Garter King at Arms, marshalled the procession, the most junior baron first and so on through the hierarchies of viscounts, earls, marquises and dukes. The mace bearer, followed by the Lord Chancellor, preceded the royal dukes, and last of all came the elegant figure of the Prince of Wales. Each man passing the empty throne made a profound bow. As the peers took their places most eyes were now turned on the small group of men who occupied the seats by the side of the accused's box. These were the impresarios of the drama that was about to begin.

For such a theatre it was appropriate that the organizers should be called 'managers'. Appropriate too, that one of them should have been a playwright, brilliant and witty. Richard Brinsley Sheridan, author of *The School for Scandal*, manager of Drury Lane, was to take the stage of Westminster Hall and populate it with characters as brittle, as insubstantial – and as fictional – as those of his own plays. It was to be excellent entertainment for the fashionable audience, and the black-market price of tickets always went up when it was known that Sheridan would speak.

It was much the same for the principal 'manager', though, as the years went by, his scurrilous rhetoric was to lose friends rather than influence people. Edmund Burke, like all great orators an actor, was now very much in need of a director's discipline. But if he did not have anyone to curb his bravura, check his timing and re-write his lines, Burke had a sort of spiritual director. Philip Francis, failed empire builder who had once fought, and lost, a duel with the accused, was called upon by Burke and the other managers to advise and assist them: not as one of the managers – the House of Commons had accepted that his hatred of the accused was too inflammatory even for those incendiary times. Then there was Charles James Fox, unusually well-dressed with bag-wig and sword, a gambler and profligate, another great orator-actor but with a warm-hearted generosity not too conspicuous among his fellow managers. Among the others, nineteen altogether, was a future governor-general of India, and the soldier-dramatist, John Burgoyne, who by losing the battle of Saratoga had helped to lose Britain's North American empire, but had not been impeached for it.

The managers stood or lounged in their places with their counsel and their shorthand writer and waited for the coming of the accused.

At exactly noon, the Sergeant-at-Arms summoned 'Warren Hastings Esq, to come forth in Court, and save thee and thy bail, otherwise the recognizance of thee and thy bail will be forfeit'. Warren Hastings, former governor-general of Fort William in Bengal, ruler of Britain's Indian dominions, came forward and having knelt at the bar was invited to rise and be seated. Many of the audience had never seen this great pro-consul before and were surprised at how small he was, just five and a half feet in height, slight in build – he had weighed himself before coming and was not surprised to find that he was only 122 lb. His suit was discreet – poppy-coloured, an eyewitness called it – and he looked thin and worn. Fanny Burney, diarist, novelist and second keeper of the robes to the Queen, found Hastings 'pale, ill and altered'. One of the managers, Sir Gilbert Elliot, later, as Lord Minto, to rule over even wider Indian dominions than Warren Hastings, thought that he had never seen 'a more miserable-looking creature', and was sure he looked 'as if he could not live a week'.

Another of the managers, William Windham, who had chosen to sit in the Ladies' Gallery next to Miss Burney, felt initially overwhelmed by 'the awfulness of the prisoner's ordeal' but quickly reminded himself of the 'thousands, the millions, who have groaned and languished under the iron rod of his oppressions'. Windham was shocked and incredulous when Miss Burney insisted that the prisoner was 'so mild, so gentle, so pleasing in his manners'. Gentle, in fact, 'even to humility'. Windham could not believe that such a monster could conceivably be humble, even if Miss Burney said so.

But these were views reflected on the retina of dislike or of friendship. Others, slightly more objective, saw Hastings dignified, pale certainly, and showing something of his suffering in his face, but also, for at least one Member of Parliament, displaying an expression at once 'bold, determined and indignant'. In reality, it was an expression of arrogant innocence which was to antagonize many.

With the accused came his counsel, Edward Law, son of a bishop and soon to be the father of a future successor to his client in the office of governor-general – the reputation Law was to gain in this trial was to take him to the high state of Lord Chief Justice – Robert Dallas, who would also one day be Lord Chief Justice and Thomas Plumer, whose speeches were as long and boring as Dallas's were witty and short. Only Dallas was without some sort of 'Indian' connection. Law's brother Thomas had been in Bengal during Hastings's administration and had profited from the governor-general's patronage. Plumer had made his name four years earlier defending Sir Thomas Rumbold, late governor of Madras, on charges of corruption and of starting an unnecessary war, almost the identical charges on which his present client now stood arraigned before the High Court of Parliament.

There were twenty-two articles of impeachment and with the separate answers of the accused they took two days to read. There was a charge that amounted to genocide: the accused had hired out troops to an Indian prince so that he might extirpate a whole people. On the accused's instigation two princesses had been harassed and their confidential servants tortured in order to make them give up their treasures. Another ruler had been goaded into rebellion by the accused's repeated demands for money and he had 'stimulated the army to rapine and outrage by the wicked orders' he had given. There were detailed charges of the taking of bribes and the granting of profitable commercial monopolies to friends and men of influence. It was a wide range of 'high crimes and misdemeanours' and the managers proposed to ensure that with bias, falsification of facts and clouds of innuendo they made of Warren Hastings the Nero and the Caligula of the age.

The trial of Warren Hastings was essentially a political trial, a matter of party rather than truth, of advantage rather than guilt. It was not the last battle for the political control of the growing British dominions in India but it was an important, even decisive incident out of which that control would ultimately emerge.

It had begun within a few days of Hastings's return from Bengal in the summer of 1785 when Edmund Burke made a cryptic remark in the House of Commons, that he would at some future time 'make a motion respecting the conduct of a gentleman just returned from India', but had done nothing by the time Parliament adjourned shortly afterwards. In Parliament there were over thirty members who had Indian interests, either through having served there themselves or through relatives in the Company's employ. Fourteen of them were closely enmeshed in the complex debts of the nawab or Arcot. There were also twenty-eight or more who were connected with the Company through shipping or investment. Among all these Hastings could number no more than five or six he could name as friends.

The situation in the Company was, to say the least, fluid. No one was in control. The three principal factions could only agree on resistance to the government. Pitt's India Act had, in fact, taken away certain of the directors' powers by creating a Board of Control to supervise the Company's affairs under the direction of a cabinet minister. The Act also gave the government a dominant voice in the appointment of governor-general. There had been clashes between the Court of Directors and the cabinet but it was the cabinet that had won. Pitt and Dundas, the two ministers most concerned with Indian affairs, disliked the Indian interest in Parliament and particularly so the friends of Hastings. In the Company they rejected Sulivan as chairman, prevented Hastings's agent Major Scott from becoming a director, and made their first appointment as governor-general, though he refused, Lord Macartney, the disobedient and basically incompetent governor of Madras. In private, Dundas showed his dislike of Hastings in more detail. He believed that the faction that supported the former governor-general was deliberately impeding the working of the Act.

Hastings seems to have gone out of his way to antagonize both Pitt and Dundas. He consulted with Thurlow, the Lord Chancellor, a distrusted but essential member of Pitt's government, trying to get the repeal of the Act or at least numerous amendments to it. An atmosphere was developing which was hardly favourable to Hastings. There was, as yet, no sign of any attempt to punish Hastings for misdeeds real or invented, but neither were there any moves to give him the honours he had a right to expect. He wanted a peerage, even an Irish one, but Pitt was adamant: the charges against Hastings made in Parliament in 1782 still stood on the resolution papers and until they were removed there could be no thought of honours.

Perhaps, then, the best move Hastings could make was to insist on some action being taken to clear his name and dispose of the old charges. Malicious gossip was massing around both him and his wife. The satires were growing in frequency and viciousness. Caricatures took up topical allusions with which to attack Hastings and his wife. A conjurer who appeared to eat stones inspired a drawing which showed the king, 'the greatest stone eater of them all', eating Hastings's diamonds and there were many others. On Hastings's request Major Scott asked Burke in the House of Commons when he intended to move the motion he had forecast in June.

Burke was delighted at this provocation. Being in opposition he was without influence and therefore without income. His creditors were beginning to cry out for payment. Burke had planned his attack on Hastings, and Scott gave him an excellent excuse to start it off with the appearance of having it forced upon him. Burke's preparations had been carefully made in conjunction with Philip Francis, who now sat in the House with Burke. But Burke had some difficulty in acquiring more allies. For one thing, his party did not believe he could succeed to the party's advantage in a House dominated by Pitt and attempts were made to persuade Burke not to take action. But he refused. He and Francis would attack together and his party would hear evidence that 'in debate they must support, or disgrace themselves for ever'.

In February 1786 Burke resurrected the resolutions of 1782 and called for the supporting papers from the government, which refused to supply them on the grounds that they were confidential. Both Pitt and Dundas were uncooperative, insisting that the material on which the resolutions were based was insufficient to justify any further action. If Burke had further charges, then of course it was a different matter. Even then, any enquiry must allow of a defence. The last Select Committee had heard only from witnesses for the prosecution. In April, Burke produced twenty-two charges buttressed in immense detail and sensed that Pitt was unwilling to risk an accusation of covering-up. Even if the House was not overly enthusiastic, Burke could feel the faint vibration of conditional acceptance. Francis was overjoyed and over-confident. In fact he believed that Hastings was 'sunk into the lowest state of misery' by the way things were going.

He was wrong, for Hastings was almost as over-confident as Francis. He was convinced that on any evidence his case would be proved to his advantage. Against the advice of all his friends except Thurlow, Hastings petitioned the House to be allowed to defend himself in person. With the aid of his friends Hastings produced his answer and on 1 May began reading it to the Commons from the bar of the House. It took several hours spread over two days to complete the 'defence' and he was assisted by two friends in the reading. Hastings certainly made some good points, but he was compelled to deal with the true gravamen of Burke's charges only superficially. Those charges took up some 400 pages and had been put together by Francis with careful quotations from state papers, documents, private letters, and the resolutions of the various Parliamentary committees. The detail was overwhelming and so carefully angled as to be almost impenetrable. Members of Parliament had been impressed, as anyone ignorant of the true circumstances would have been. Each point really needed to be discussed and corrected. Hastings could only deal with them briefly.

In his introductory remarks he outlined what he had tried to do in India and the difficulties that had faced him, difficulties 'which are unknown to the rulers and ministers of other governments'. Not only that, but he had often found himself opposed and his 'conduct circumscribed by orders which would apply to few cases which occurred, and those orders uncertain in their construction'. The defence of the 'unique situation' is never particularly effective but he felt that it had to be pointed out.

'Under such circumstances I humbly apprehend that since it is not . . . the lot of human nature to be exempt from error, some notorious calamity . . . or some well-ascertained ground of corruption or other moral deviation from my duty, the loss of national reputation, or of substantial property, ought to have appeared' before he was subject to impeachment. And yet no such thing had been presented by his accusers. 'What losses has the nation sustained through my mismanagement? Have provinces been dismembered from it? Have its armies been defeated in operations of my formation? Or war or famine wasted the countries of my jurisdiction?' On the contrary. He had saved British India and now was being 'punished before conviction' by unsubstantiated abuse.

Hastings left the House confident that he had succeeded in repelling the charges. 'My credit stands higher by many degrees than it ever did.' His appearance was followed by several days of evidence given by people involved in one way or another with the charges. Though many of them were severely handled by Burke, the general consensus of their evidence was not to Hastings's disadvantage. When the first debate opened on 1 June, Dundas opposed a motion for impeachment claiming that since the offence – the Rohilla war – Hastings had three times been reappointed governor-general, which amounted to a pardon anyway. The motion was lost by 119 votes to 67. Hastings and many of his friends chose to believe that this would be the end of the affair, but they misunderstood the motives of both Burke and Francis. Burke was determined to use Indian affairs as a pathway to power. Francis intended to continue a campaign that had begun twelve years before in the Council chamber at Calcutta.

On 13 June the subject for debate was Chait Singh and Banaras. When the members voted it was 119 to 79 – for impeachment. The responsibility now lay with Pitt. When he rose to dissect the speech of Fox, the House was rewarded with a demolition of Fox's arguments. Pitt accepted Hastings's assessment of the position of Chait Singh. He was not, said Pitt, the independent prince of Fox and the rest of the opposition but a landholder in tributary relationship with the Company. Hastings had every right to punish him with a fine. Then the tone of Pitt's voice changed: 'But in proposing to inflict a fine of (5 million) rupees, Hastings had set a penalty utterly disproportionate to the offence, and therefore disgracefully exorbitant'. In consequence Pitt was compelled to find him 'deserving of censure upon this point'.

The House was astonished. Members of Pitt's party who had come prepared to vote against the motion, followed their leaders into the 'yes' lobby. With one speech Pitt had brought the impeachment of Warren Hastings. It was of no consequence that the 'exorbitant' fine had never been collected, that in Hastings's own words he had 'been declared guilty of a high crime and misdemeanour in having *intended* to exact a fine too large for the offence . . .' To be justified in imposing a fine but condemned for imposing one too high but not enforced, seemed like madness. Why, then, did Pitt act as he did? There have been many suggestions – the influence of Dundas, who saw in Hastings a potential rival in the management of Indian affairs, being the most popular. But it is not acceptable. It is much more likely that Pitt was manoeuvring to maintain his majority, split into factions, for what he believed to be more important matters than the impeachment of Warren Hastings of whom he really did not approve anyway. In this Hastings was a victim of party politics.

It was to be eighteen months before the preliminaries of impeachment were disposed of. Immediately after the Banaras vote, Parliament went into recess and on its return it continued its debates until April 1787. Francis was everywhere, joining in the debates, supplying others with information and trying to get more himself from India. It was not only Hastings who was to be impeached; Elijah Impey was also attacked, and whatever the outcome Francis was sure the trial would 'gibbet their characters to eternity'.

In February 1787, the charge of exploiting the Begums of

Oudh came before the House. During the debate Richard Brinsley Sheridan delighted the members and the distinguished guests in the galleries with a display of his dramatic art. He had, Burke said, 'a sort of love passion for the Begums'. He described the princesses, gentle and reserved, harassed by cruel soldiers, their servants tortured. Hastings was a 'trickster and a tyrant', a 'felon kite'. As for Impey, 'ferreting with affidavits', he was almost as bad. When Sheridan sat down there was applause from the gallery and a substantial adversary vote from the members. Pitt once again voted for the motion, and so did many others who were convinced by Sheridan, 'though some did so with pain'.

The tide was now definitely against Hastings and there could be no turning back. Burke even suggested that he should be arrested in case he fled the country. Hostile witnesses increased in number, quoting dead men without question, blackening Hastings's character with hearsay. Other charges were carried. By April the only question that seemed to need settling was which charges would form the main basis of the impeachment and the fixing of the day of the trial. On 10 May Burke took the charges to the House of Lords and eleven days later Hastings was taken into custody by the sergeant-at-arms, passed on to Black Rod and taken to the bar of the Lords. There he was required to kneel, 'a punishment', he described it, 'not only before conviction, but before the accusations'. After this, Hastings was not required to appear until late in November.

On 6 February, Hastings went to see the preparations at Westminster Hall where the trial was to be held and where in a week's time he would be compelled to appear 'as a criminal'. In that week's time, too, though he did not know it, was to begin an ordeal that would last for eight years.

The longest and most notorious political trial in British history inflicted on the accused a double ordeal. There were the sessions themselves, full of almost obscene malice tearing at the flesh with barbed words and phrases, and there were the spaces in between raw with uncertainty and foreboding. The actual proceedings were in fact short. In the opening year of 1788 the session lasted for 35 days; in 1789, 17; 1790, 14; 1791 only 5; 1792 and 1793, 22 in each; 1794, 28; and those of the final year of 1795 throughout the months of January to April. The prosecution did not complete its case until May 1791 and the defence in the same month of 1793. The remaining two years were spent in quasi-judicial wranglings over the recall of witnesses and of conflicts between the two Houses of Parliament. During the years of trial, a third of the House of Lords died, and when the verdict came to be given only twenty-nine peers who had attended continuously were called upon to cast their vote. Some witnesses were not called at all, most of them for the defence.

The reasons for this apparently extraordinary prolongation of proceedings lay partly in the nature of the court itself. Parliament seldom sat for more than five or six months of the year, the judges were often away on circuit, and the Lords felt that they could not do without them. There was also the business of Parliament itself, and during the years much of this was pressing. There was the problem of the king's madness and of the Regency, the ever-widening consequences of the revolution in France which led to war in 1793. The trial was fitted into what time could be spared from the affairs of the nation.

1788
Burke's opening speech lasted four days. As a work of art it had form, unity, contrast, colour, and, above all, imagination. He treated his hearers to a survey of India's history which bore little relation to the facts. Burke was not concerned with instructing his audience, but with turning them against the accused. He played upon their emotions, drawing for them a magnificent picture of a Bengal flowing with the good things of life, and the wonders of a great civilization blighted by the descent on it of Hastings and his bandits. He sketched a powerful contrast between the men of honour, Francis, Clavering and Monson,

and the immoral Hastings, whom he charged with fraud, abuse of power, robbery, treachery, murder, 'with cruelties unheard of and devastations almost without name'. He accused Hastings of 'crimes which have their rise in the wicked dispositions of men – in avarice, rapacity, cruelty, malignity of temper, haughtiness, insolence – in short, in everything that manifests a heart blackened to the very blackest – a heart dyed in blackness – a heart gangrened to the core . . . We have brought before you the head, the chief, the captain-general of iniquity – one in whom all the fraud, all the tyranny of India are embodied, disciplined and arrayed'. The charges were manifold. The accused had 'taken away the lands of orphans'. He had alienated the fortunes of widows', 'wasted the country, and destroyed the inhabitants after cruelly harassing and distressing them'. Burke charged Hastings with 'having tortured their persons, and dishonoured their religion through his wicked agents, who were at the bottom and root of his villainy'. He had 'gorged his ravenous maw', 'feeding on the indigent, the dying and ruined' like the 'ravenous vulture who destroys and incapacitates nature in the destruction of its object while devouring the carcases of the dead'. Hastings, Burke revealed, was a man of pretence, 'a swindling Maecenas'. And all was a part with his origin, which was 'low, obscure and vulgar'.

As Burke warmed to his subject he referred to 'the damned and damnable proceedings of a judge in Hell' and asserted that 'such a judge was Warren Hastings'. The English language 'does not afford terms adequate to the enormity of his offences'. Finally the great flow of words came to an end in an appeal to impeach the 'common enemy and oppressor of us all'. It was a most impressive performance. Hastings himself declared that 'for half an hour I looked up at the orator in a reverie of wonder, and actually felt myself the most culpable man. But,' he added, 'I recurred to my own bosom, and there found a consciousness which consoled me under all I heard, and all I suffered'.

Burke set the style and the others followed. Fox was quieter but the attack was sharp-edged. Another of the 'managers', Charles Grey, following Burke, referred in ringing tones to the terrible 'enormities' of the accused: 'Outrage, exaction, devastation and death! the distress of nations! all nature blasted by the withering malignity of man! the helpless and the unoffending. O what is useful what is honourable – the peasant and the prince – all prematurely swept together to the grave!' The dialogue of a vast and bloody drama echoed through Westminster Hall, exciting the anger of the peers and frightening the fashionable ladies into tears and fainting.

But the managers did not get their way in the matter of procedure. They wished to take each charge separately, producing the evidence and questioning witnesses, hearing the defence and then calling for judgement on each. Hastings's counsel argued that it would be grossly unfair to the accused. To rebut one charge it would often be necessary to reveal the general line of the defence which could then be prepared for by the prosecution. On this the House decided in favour of Hastings. The managers claimed that the High Court of Parliament 'should not be fettered by those rules of law which prevail in inferior courts'. The law of slander should not apply within its walls nor should any evidence, however circumstantial, be ruled out. This, too, the Lords rejected.

The first charge, opened by Fox, concerned Chait Singh of Banaras. Fox reminded the members of the court of their duty to uphold the honour of England in the eyes of a closely watching world. But the rhetoric had to give way to the duller areas of evidence. The fireworks dampened, the fashionable audience took itself to less boring pleasures. The examination of witnesses – all for the prosecution – was tedious in the extreme except when by accident evidence was given that supported the defence. This was dismissed by the managers as the result of years of brain-washing by the accused! When the matter of Chait Singh had been disposed of, it was time for the charge concerning the spolation of the Begums of Oudh. The taking of evidence lasted for sixteen days. Among the witnesses was Impey whose personal defence aroused Burke: 'O miserable state of the East India Company,' he declaimed, 'O abandoned fortune of Mr Hastings! O fallen lot of England! When no assistance could be found but what was given by Sir Elijah Impey!'

The evidence, however carefully angled and confused by rhetoric, would just not sustain the managers' case that Hastings had conspired to rob the Begums, then forced the nawab to act on his behalf against them, and then created a story to cover up his acts.

Between the acts of his tragedy, Sheridan produced interludes of uplifting homily. Their effect upon the audience was considerable. One of the managers, Gilbert Elliot, could not recollect ever crying 'so heartily and copiously on any public occasion'. 'Filial Piety! It is the primal bond of society!' 'It is the sacrament of nature, not only the duty but the indulgence of man.' 'It is his first great privilege. It is among his last most enduring delights! When the bosom glows with the idea of reverberated love – when to requite on the visitations of nature, and return the blessings that have been received! When – what emotion fixed into vital principle – what was instinct habituated into master-passion – sway all the sweetest energies of man – hangs over each vicissitude of all that must pass away, to cheer the langours of decrepitude and age, explore the thought, explain the aching eye!'

The incoherence of the printed word was certainly not apparent in the actor's verbal delivery. Sheridan had his audience suspending reality and caught in the make-believe world he had created for them. 'O Faith! O Justice! I conjure you by your sacred names to depart for a moment from this place . . .' When speaking of the accused such virtues were banished, unable to exist along with the 'long catalogue of crimes and aggravations, beyond the reach of thought for human malignity to perpetuate, or human vengeance to punish, lower than perdition – blacker than despair!' Edward Gibbon, author of the first volumes of a study of decline and fall of an earlier empire than that of the British, was present in Westminster Hall and commented on the end of Sheridan's speech: 'at the close . . . [he] sunk into Burke's arms, but I called this morning; he is perfectly well - a good actor'.

1789

The rhetoric was of the same quality as the year before but the hatred of the managers for the accused seemed, if anything, to have intensified. When Hastings complained that the slowness of the trial was ruining him financially, Burke replied that it was one way of reducing the immense fortune Hastings had made in India. The subject of the next charge was the acceptance of bribes. 'The crimes which are laid to the charge of Mr Hastings,' said Burke, 'are of the grovelling kind, which do not grow upon a throne, but are hatched in dunghills.' 'He was a vulture fattening upon carrion. He lay down in his style of infamy wallowing in the filth of disgrace – and fattening upon the offals and excrements of dishonour!' It was during one of these calculated invectives that Robert Dallas, one of Hastings's defence counsel, passed to his client an epigram which was later to become famous:

> Oft have I wondered that in Irish Ground
> No poisonous reptiles ever yet were found;
> Reveal'd the secret strands of nature's work,
> She sav'd her venom to create a Burke.

In this session the managers went too far and tried to introduce the affair of Nand Kumar which was not a subject of charges against Hastings. This did not worry Burke, who in April accused Hastings of murdering Nand Kumar 'by the hands of Elijah Impey'. Hastings appealed to the House of Commons against the introduction of material not in the charges and was justified by a substantial vote in his favour. Burke and his friends, however, continued to refer to the 'murder' of Nand Kumar. 'No matter,' cried Burke, 'the charge is true, though I am forbidden to say so.'

1790

The next session was still concerned with the matter of bribes. The witnesses called rather bolstered the defence case than the opposite. Fox did his best: 'if I do not clearly prove all these particulars upon his head,' he thundered, 'may the arm of that God they have invoked fall heavily upon me, and make me the living scorn of man, the striking monument of his anger, whose attribute is Truth, and from whom the punishment of Falsehood is assured'. God took no action, even though Fox failed to prove his case.

1791

Before the session opened a new Commons had been elected and there were questions of constitutional propriety to be settled. Perhaps the impeachment had died with the old Parliament? Hastings's supporters insisted that it had, but it was the managers who won. To protests that the trial had already gone on too long, Burke replied that those who thought so were no more capable of knowing what ought to be the length of an impeachment 'than a rabbit, which breeds six times a year, is capable of judging the time of gestation of an elephant'. As a concession Burke agreed to drop a number of charges. The main points at issue in this section were: (1) a corrupt contract for the sale of opium given in 1781 to Lawrence Sulivan's son Stephen; (2) an alleged attempt by Hastings to smuggle opium into China; (3) a contract for the supply of draft animals for the army; (4) the granting of illegal allowances to Eyre Coote; (5) an agency for supplies given to a Mr Auriol in Madras; and (6) another given to a Mr Belli for provisions for Fort William, Calcutta.

These were the weakest of all the charges and the evidence produced was most unsatisfactory. But at least it was the end of the case for the prosecution. On the last day of the session, the accused rose to open his defence. He had maintained an almost stoic silence throughout the seventy-three days of the trial so far, except for an occasion or two when the malignant absurdity of some remark had driven him to interrupt, as on the occasion when one of the managers had opened on the second charge, that concerning the Begums of Oudh, and Hastings had murmured: 'It is a lie,' and received an angry response: 'What! Shall I hear, my Lords, and bear that my assertion shall be contradicted? Shall I, who stand here as the delegated manager of the Commons, be told that I am advancing what is untrue? In the situation in which I stand – and from that degraded man at your bar, loaded with crimes, and groaning under his enormities, I will not bear it.'

Hastings's defence was simple and, in direct contrast with the tone of his accusers, moderate and reasoned. He asked what he was to do about witnesses for his defence. He had been denied swift justice and many were now dead. Would he now be allowed to enter their sworn affidavits? He had come to answer charges, not to be reviled. When he had produced testimonials from India they were dismissed by Burke as 'yet warm from the thumbscrews' as if 'injured people' rose up 'voluntarily to bear false testimony in favour of a distant and persecuted oppressor'.

Hastings apologized for the fact that, unlike his accusers, he was no orator and was compelled to read from notes. On one occasion when interrupted he cried out 'save me from this violence, I beseech you do not let me be interrupted. I cannot speak from the sudden impulse of my own mind'. But he could still make good points. He had maintained 'the provinces of my immediate administration in a state of peace, plenty and fecundity, when every other member of the British Empire was involved in external wars or civil tumult' – a timely reminder of the loss of the American colonies. He had not cost the Company

167

or the state money needed elsewhere, but had raised the revenue from 'three to five millions sterling, not of a temporary and forced exaction, but of an early, continued, and still existing production, the best evidence of a good government – improving agriculture and increased population'.

In reply to the accusation that he had desolated the provinces of British India, he dared to reply that 'they are . . . the most flourishing of all the States of India'. It was he, Hastings, who had made them so. 'The valour of others acquired, I enlarged and gave them shape and consistency to the dominion you hold there: I preserved it; I sent forth its armies with an effectual but economic hand . . . I maintained the wars which were of your formation, or that of others, not mine . . . When you cried out for peace, and your cries were heard by those who were the objects of it, I resisted this and every other species of counteraction by rising in my demands, and accomplished a peace, and I hope a lasting one, with one great state; and I at least afforded the efficient means by which a peace, if not so durable, more seasonable at least was accomplished with another. I gave you all; and you have rewarded me with confiscation, disgrace and a life of impeachment.'

1792

There was no way of stopping the inexorable but slow movement of the proceedings of impeachment, even Hastings's willingness to waive his defence in return for a quick vote and an end to the affair. The trial had lost much of its appeal even to the peers who were to judge it. The fashionable world had become tired of the vulgarity of Burke's abuse. Only Burke and Francis seemed undimmed in their hatred and determination to continue with the attack. The defence counsel, too, seemed to perpetuate the proceedings with long-winded speeches. But some of the witnesses were having their effect. John Shore, a man of obvious integrity, radiating impartiality, when asked whether Hastings were the corrupt and cruel figure painted by the prosecution he would continue to be on friendly terms with him, replied, 'I should hope not'. William Markham, after telling evidence in the matter of Chait Singh, declared he was 'convinced, my Lords, Mr Hastings is the most virtuous man of the age in which he lives', and the feeling of the Court now seemed to be with him.

1793

Yet still the trial dragged on with Burke and the managers denying any need for haste. Frequently there were not enough peers present to properly constitute the court. But it was in this session that the defence was finally closed, and on the last day of the session the accused addressed the court:

'In the presence of that Being from whom no secrets are hid, I do, upon a full review and scrutiny of my past life, unequivocally and conscientiously declare, that in the administration of that trust of government, which was so many years confided in me, I did in no instance intentionally sacrifice the interest of my country to any private views of my personal advantage; that according to my best skill and judgement, I invariably promoted the essential interest of my employers, the happiness and prosperity of the people committed to my charge and the honour and welfare of my country, and at no time with more entire devotion of mind and purpose to these objects, than during the period in which my accusers have endeavoured to represent me as occupied and engrossed by the base pursuits of low, sordid and interdicted emolument.'

As the defence now rested, the Lords were anxious to get to the verdicts, but the managers said they were not ready and another year was allowed to pass.

1794

The new session opened with arguments about inadmissible

evidence, but in April the spectacle came to life again. At Hastings's request his successor as governor-general, Lord Cornwallis, gave testimony on revenue matters and the question of Oudh. The evidence given by Cornwallis was brief and shattering. He did not believe that the Begums had been hounded into poverty or anything like it, nor that there was anything for anybody to be ashamed of in Hastings's treatment of Chait Singh. As for his conduct of the great war, Hastings had rendered 'essential services'. In the matter of the revenue, Cornwallis had heard no complaints and Hastings 'was much esteemed and respected' by Indians.

Cornwallis was followed by William Larkins, the late accountant-general whom Cornwallis described as 'a man whose knowledge, abilities and acknowledged integrity entitled everything that came from him to the fullest consideration'. Even under Burke's cross-examination Larkins was firm. Hastings's handling of financial matters was honest and he had been 'perfectly careless as to the state of his own private fortune'.

There now seemed some firm chance of acquittal, though the managers were once again allowed to prolong the proceedings. Hastings's financial position was now nearly desperate. Burke still fulminated and when Hastings interrupted his last speech to deny an assertion, Burke referred to him as a 'wicked wretch' and his defence as the ravings of an 'unhappy man' who ought 'to be sent to Bridewell'. There was nothing, it seemed, that could quiet the hatred of Burke. He surpassed his previous speeches in foul language and he pleaded that it was not 'the culprit who is on trial, it is the House of Commons that is upon its trial, it is the House of Lords that is upon its trial, it is the British nation that is upon its trial before all other nations, before the present generation, and before a long, long posterity'.

In June the Lords withdrew to consider the case and the Commons returned to their own place where Pitt moved a vote of thanks to the managers. An attempt was made to exclude Burke from the vote. He had lost many friends during the years and was now a lonely and somewhat tragic figure, who had made his last appearance in the House and in two years would be dead.

It was not until 23 April 1795 that the members of the House of Lords went in procession for the last time to the court-room of Westminster Hall. Once again the public galleries were crowded. No member of the royal family was present though *The Times* recorded that the Princess of Wales had intended to go after receiving a formal address of congratulation on her marriage from the Corporation of the City of London, but the trial was over by the time she was free.

From early March until the final day, the arguments and discussion in the Lords had been dominated by Lord Thurlow. He had all the complicated matters of the long proceedings at his fingertips and was quick to point out the essential elements of failure in the managers' case. On fourteen of the charges no evidence had been offered at all and the others carried the seeds of their own dismissal. Thurlow particularly concentrated on those dealing with financial corruption and his analysis was warmly welcomed by the twenty-nine peers who would finally vote. The rest of the Lords, those who for a variety of reasons had not heard a substantial part of the case, would abstain.

At 12.30 the accused was called in, and once more kneeling at the bar, he was ordered to rise and then asked to leave the court. The Lord Chancellor, Lord Loughborough, then put sixteen questions to each of the twenty-nine peers, who were wearing their robes. Was the prisoner Guilty or Not Guilty? The vote was for acquittal on every charge. On the two most serious, that of Chait Singh and of the Begums of Oudh, the vote was twenty-three to six. On the various charges of corruption the vote against Hastings was never more than five. On the final charge, 'That he was guilty of other high crimes and misdemeanours', the voting was: Not Guilty, 25; Guilty, 4. At this there was a round of applause from the visitors and the prisoner was called in to hear the final verdict. Hastings bowed respectfully to the court and left.

Hastings was now sixty-three and very nearly bankrupt. Six of his friends from India each lent him £2,000 in 1795 and he had another £3,000 on loan from another old friend. During the years 1790–1, £17,000 had been produced in contributions from the Company's employees in India. But this was a small sum to set against his debts. The trial itself cost over £70,000 of which £40,000 was still outstanding at 5 per cent interest. His total indebtedness could not be less than £90,000. His assets included the estate at Daylesford, which he finally acquired after the death of its owner in 1788, a valuable diamond and shares in two East Indiamen.

Hastings believed that it was the state that owed him reimbursement. His legal advisers were not so sure. But Hastings went ahead with a petition which he sent to the Prime Minister with a request that he submit it to the king. Pitt replied in a short formal note that he did not feel able to justify such an act. Hastings's friends urged him to lay his case before the Court of Directors and to demand that the Company defray his expenses. Hastings was unwilling; his claim, he insisted, was 'against the British Nation'. The Company's chairman, Stephen Lushington, put two proposals before his fellow directors. The first was that Hastings's legal expenses should be met by the Company, and the second that he should be given an annuity of £5,000. A similar sum had in fact been granted to Cornwallis. The directors were by no means unanimous, though the proposals were accepted by ballot. There was still a certain amount of moral disapproval of Hastings's policies.

Some delay was caused by the doubtful legal position of the Company under the new India Act. It was not clear that the directors had the right to indemnify Hastings out of Indian revenues. The atmosphere was not lightened by an ill-advised letter from Hastings who now seemed to believe that it was his right to claim costs from the Company and that 'this was less my trial than that of the East India Company and the British Nation'. When the directors referred the matter to the Board of Control it was decided that payment to Hastings would come under the head of extraordinary financial grants, and thus subject to government approval. Hastings noted in his journal: 'my disappointment on Thursday caused me to lose my temper and affected me the whole day'.

The government's reply was unfavourable. But Hastings's friends continued to put pressure both on the Company and on the Board, and in April an agreement was reached between the directors and the president of the Board, Henry Dundas. The Company was permitted to grant Hastings an annuity of £4,000 for a period of $28\frac{1}{2}$ years dating from his return in 1785 and ending with the expiry of the Company's existing Charter in 1813, and a loan free of interest of £50,000. This meant that he would receive both the loan and an immediate sum of £42,000 for his annuity up to date. On the surface, it appeared generous, though it was less than that voted to Cornwallis. But the Company insisted that £2,000 a year be kept back to reduce the principal on the loan and that the title deeds of Daylesford be assigned as security. As Hastings estimated his yearly expenditure as £3,500, 'rather below than exceeding the rank in life which my former station might have entitled me to assume', and would have to produce another £1,000 in interest on another debt, he could only move steadily into bankruptcy. Three years later, when in fact he did find his debts increasing, he asked the Company to grant him compound interest on the £2,000 deducted by them annually. This they agreed to do.

Hastings was never to be free from financial difficulties but many of these were due to a mixture of generosity and recklessness, the latter particularly so in the expenditure on the estate at Daylesford. But Hastings's shortage of cash after the end of the impeachment did not mean that he had not made a fortune out of India.

Though Hastings was by no means a typical nabob, he had not

neglected opportunities available to him. It would have been surprising if he had. Even Lord North, it was said, thought it would have been quite reasonable for Hastings to have left India with a fortune of £200,000. When he finally resigned his post, Hastings did so with a fortune less than a third of that sum. But there had been substantial profits in the past. In the first four years of his administration, when his salary had been £25,000 a year, he had remitted to England sums amounting to £122,000! After 1775, Hastings found even his enormous salary did not cover his expenses and got into debt. Even so, in his last ten years, his remittances home amounted to £96,000, so producing a total of £218,000. Unfortunately, Hastings's generosity to relatives and friends and his heavy political expenses in London meant that by 1785 only £75,000 was left.

That Hastings did not make better use of his opportunities for profit was in part due to the depth of his devotion to his duties as governor-general, to the interests of the Company and to his belief in the historic importance of what he was trying to do in India. Making a very large fortune demands *personal* attention, and this Hastings chose not to give to his financial affairs. In fact, his agents in England were constantly warning him of the confusion in his personal finances. Though himself uncorrupt, Hastings's attitude to money was, in the words of Charles James Fox, 'peculiarly magnificent'. He rewarded his friends and those who might be helpful to him extravagantly. He would give one absentee head of the Revenue Board £15,000 a year; to another friend an opium contract which was promptly sold for £40,000. And to retain Eyre Coote's support and services he was prepared to be more than generous. The sums were large, the accounting of them vague in the extreme.

Hastings never tried to conceal, more than temporarily, these dispersals of the sums he himself received from a wide variety of sources, most of them tainted. He was often secretive about them – this he claimed was absolutely necessary when he was in a minority in Council. He believed implicitly that what he did was dictated by the demands of the state, for whose administration he was responsible. The explanation was simple. He behaved as an Indian ruler in an Indian political environment, and his morality was that of the situation he found himself in. It was an excuse that might have been put forward by any of the lesser men who had profited from India. Their day was now at an end, for the successor to Warren Hastings as governor-general had been specifically ordered to anglicize the rule of the British in India and to stamp out corruption wherever it was to be found.

[II] *Into Myth and History*

Hastings left Calcutta in February 1785, and it was not until September 1787 that his successor arrived in Bengal. The interregnum had been presided over by John Macpherson, whose stewardship had left 'a government rendered contemptible from its imbecility; all confidence in its measures or abilities destroyed, and private and public credit depreciated'. As for Macpherson's administration, 'a total want of energy, dignity and common sense distinguished it. Evasion was substituted for decision; caution and hesitation instead of action'. And that was the mildest of criticisms. Another described the situation as displaying only 'meanness, timidity, injustice, tyranny, weakness, ignorance, fickelness . . .'

The situation facing Lord Cornwallis, who had only with reluctance accepted the post, giving up a 'life of ease and content' for what he was sure were to be 'all the plagues and miseries of command and public station', was not appealing.

Cornwallis brought with him a number of qualifications; a strong sense of duty, a military reputation that had not suffered from his defeat at Yorktown during the American War of Independence, and, not least, no previous experience of India. He also came armed with more powers than his predecessor. He could override his own Council whenever he chose and combined the powers of governor-general with those of commander-in-chief. Above all, he had something Hastings had never had – the complete confidence of the government at home, and of the directors of the East India Company.

Cornwallis's instruction from the directors of the Company was to institute an enquiry into the actions of its employees, on every level, whom it believed were defrauding the Company of its just profits. If investigations should lead Cornwallis to suspect anyone of fraud, he was to suspend all such offenders from their employment. If charges were proved, the guilty must make restitution and return to England within a year of judgement against them. The problem Cornwallis found, was not so much identifying the wrongdoers but in obtaining legal proof of their wrongdoing. 'The customs and prejudices of the natives,' Cornwallis wrote, 'render it difficult in such cases to obtain information from them.' Nevertheless, he was moderately successful and, with new men and reforms in the system, Cornwallis was able to claim by the end of 1788 that abuses in the Commercial Department, that original 'sink of corruption and iniquity' had disappeared.

Cornwallis was convinced, as was Hastings before him, that the best way to remove temptation from the Company's servants was to pay them a salary substantial enough to ensure their probity. At the same time it was necessary to prohibit *all* Company employees from trading. Cornwallis did not, however, think that a total ban could be made to work at that time, and it was to be many years before it was.

Among Cornwallis's more marked successes was the removal of the worst abuses of patronage. Up until his time, the Company's service was regarded as a source of employment for relatives, friends, and political supporters of the ruling class as well as anyone who might have rendered a service or who needed to be bought off. Cornwallis rejected requests for posts from the highest in the land, including the queen and the prince of Wales. By 1787, Sir John Shore, Hastings's friend, informed him that 'the system of patronage which you so justly reprobated, and which you always found so grievous a tax, had been entirely subverted'. Shore was a little premature, but the abuse was much decreased.

Cornwallis sailed from India (handing over to Shore) in 1793. He left behind an Augean stables swept reasonably clean. Fraud and embezzlement had – almost – become things of the past in all departments, and the general quality of the Company's employees had enormously improved. The nabob might still be around, but 'nabobery' had ceased to exist. Though not in popular mythology.

One of the most enduring of myths is that of the malign influence of the greed of the nabobs upon Bengal and its inhabitants. Surely these men could not have acquired great fortunes except by plundering Bengal into ruin! But did they? Unfortunately, there is very little data concerning many aspects of the social and economic history of Bengal in the eighteenth century. Men like Edmund Burke and Philip Francis were convinced that there was a 'drain of wealth' from Bengal which only profited private persons.

Francis believed that the 'drain' was a combination of Company taxation and private exploitation. He compared the Company's territories in India with the Asiatic provinces of the Roman empire before Augustus: 'In the time of Cicero the Romans were treating their provinces in Asia as we have treated ours. They taxed with one hand and monopolised with the other. They demanded from their subjects an exorbitant revenue which they made impossible to pay, first by engrossing the produce of the lands, in character of proprietor, and then by appropriating the trade and industry of the people in quality of merchant.'

The rhetoric of Francis sounded all very fine, in the House of Commons, and with £500,000 a year on private account being received in Britain between 1757 and 1784 it might seem true as well. But most of the money was transferred from India to Britain in the form of bills-of-exchange payable in London while the actual cash remained in Bengal to defray the Company's military and civil expenses.

The role of the British in the general economy of Bengal was not overwhelming, though they entrenched themselves in certain areas which they believed to be particularly profitable. Even then, Indian merchants were by no means excluded. Indeed, there was much collaboration. Many Indians were enriched by the British conquest of Bengal, though ordinary people – as usual – do not seem to have benefited. However, it would not appear that any serious damage was caused by the nabobs' desire for profit. It would also seem that little constructive resulted either. But there were side-effects and momentous ones at that.

The nabobs had considered themselves merchants. Their purpose was to get rich before climate and disease got them. As long as they did not cheat their employers too much, they believed they were entitled to make their fortunes. Out of their pursuit of private profit in Bengal came territorial empire and commercial leadership in India. The line between growing British power in India and private profit is obvious if not precise. The 'revolutions' in Bengal which led to direct rule by the British brought enormous profits and advantage to those who grasped the potentialities. Presents, prize-money, trading rights, all came in a deluge of profit from a dabble in politics. But fundamental changes in the *source* of power were not susceptible to private greed. It was the *Company* that demanded more and more privileges until it finally took all of the power for itself.

When the nabobs were all but forgotten, there remained their spirit of free enterprise. In fact, a partnership grew up between the East India Company and private entrepreneurs. The Company, for example, took monopoly control of the production of salt, saltpetre and opium, leaving such things as sugar, indigo and raw silk, to which were later added tea and jute, to private enterprise. With this economic activity came banks and other financial institutions to service it and to channel investment. The growth of British dominion, first in India and then in Asia, was a direct consequence of that partnership. The nabobs may not have known – did not know – what they were starting.

But they did know what they wanted to do with their fortunes. Generally speaking, they spent their money on houses and land, and invested in government stock to ensure themselves a steady income. They do not seem – as has been suggested – to have contributed much if anything to the resources, the capital accumulation, which was to fuel the Industrial Revolution. Only one nabob, Claud Alexander, the Company's paymaster-general, who left Bengal in 1785, seems to have ventured in any substantial way into industry on his return to Britain. He opened a cotton mill and founded a new town in Ayrshire, though even he, like the others, preferred to be a country landowner.

Among the hard-headed, single-minded men of trade and profit, one nabob, at least, towers above the commonplace. Warren Hastings did not spend all his time in India amassing a fortune or fighting his own people and Indian rulers. Among all the diversions he made the effort to understand India, the country, the people, and their civilization. In doing so, he made a lasting contribution to the general culture of mankind.

Hastings's interest in the culture of the country in which he worked had begun early. In 1762 he had pictures and books sent down from Patna and had begun to build up a library which, when it was eventually sold to the Company, contained nearly 200 volumes in Persian and Arabic as well as others in Sanskrit and Hindi. The Persian and Arabic manuscripts included works on history and medicine and much poetry, some magnificently illuminated. There was also a collection of Mughal and Persian miniatures. That Hastings understood and loved Muslim culture is confirmed by his interest in criticizing works of poetry and by an abortive project for the establishment of a professorship of Persian at Oxford.

After his appointment to Bengal, Hastings was able to give his interest a practical expression. In his concern for indigenous law he encouraged the translation of legal works. Nathaniel Halhed produced an English version of a digest of Hindu laws which was published in England in 1776. Halhed knew no Sanskrit and his translation was made from an edition in Persian. It was to be the first of a series of translations, all with the active patronage and encouragement of the governor-general. They were the beginnings of modern oriental scholarship. After Halhed came Charles Wilkins, who quickly mastered Sanskrit and whose translation of the *Bhagavad-gita* was the first scholarly version of a Hindu classic to appear in print in any European language. Wilkins referred to Hastings as his 'preceptor and patron' and it was through Hastings's friendly relations with Hindu pandits – notoriously secretive with most Europeans – that access to texts and commentary had been possible.

Towards the end of Hastings's period of office in India, there arrived in Bengal one of the remarkable men of the eighteenth century. Sir William Jones was a famous literary figure in London in the early 1770s. He had mastered Arabic, Persian, Latin, Greek, French, Italian, German, Spanish, Portuguese, some Hebrew and a little Chinese by the time he had reached his middle twenties. His first book was a *Grammar of the Persian Language*. Finding academic life boring, he then obtained appointment as a judge of the Bengal Supreme Court and arrived in Calcutta in December 1783.

Hastings and Jones became firm friends, even though Jones was an intimate of Edmund Burke. It was the arrival of such a scholar as Jones that seemed to crown the work of Hastings and his small group of orientalists and it was celebrated in the founding of the Asiatic Society. Jones was to spend ten years in India, dying there at the early age of forty-eight. But the work he did was to transform the European view of India.

The respect all these men felt for Hastings and for the patronage which had made their work possible was expressed while he was at Banaras during the wet season of 1784. Charles Wilkins, who had just completed his translation of the *Bhagavad-gita*, asked Hastings to write an introduction. Wilkins in his own preface praised the constant help Hastings had given to

Company servants in the study of languages and their literatures. In his introduction Hastings praised the work of its translator. Such works as the *Gita* would live 'when the British dominion in India has long ceased to exist'. The *Gita* contained passages 'elevated to a track of sublimity into which our habits of judgement will find it difficult to pursue'.

Perhaps the most fascinating revelation of Hastings's personality – and one that is not irrelevant in our illiberal age – emerges from what he was *unable* to achieve: a reconciliation of Europe and India. That the attempt was made at all has often been obscured by the propaganda of anti-colonialism and the harsh apartheid of the imperial heyday. Hastings's cultural curiosity was characteristic of the eighteenth century, but his enthusiasm for oriental scholarship was not. In the first, Hastings's interests were wide. His garden at Alipur was full of 'curious and valuable exotics from all quarters' and an inspiration for the systematic examination of Indian flora. When he sent George Bogle to Tibet in 1774, Bogle's instructions were to collect information on everything from polyandry to cooking!

Hastings's enthusiastic patronage of oriental scholarship had a practical as well as an intellectual base. He believed that India should be ruled in traditional ways and that those British set in authority should speak Indian languages, understand Indian laws and customs. Such knowledge would contribute to the facility, as well as the stability, of British rule, just as his horticultural and agricultural experiments would result in new commercial products, and the expeditions to Tibet in an increase in external trade.

Hastings, however, saw the function of oriental scholarship in less immediately practical terms. He believed that it would 'open our minds' and that translations from 'every branch of Indian literature' would enrich 'the stock of European knowledge'. There is no doubt that Hastings's own literary tastes were involved and that he enjoyed the status of patron, but his own letters reveal that he had a much deeper purpose. He called it a plan 'for the reconciliation of the people of England to the natives of Hindustan'. Indians would understand and accept British rule if they realized that their rulers respected and admired their religion, their laws and their institutions. The British at home would learn to accept their Indian subjects by understanding their laws, religion and institutions. 'Every instance which brings their real character home to observation will impress us with a more generous sense of feeling for their natural rights, and teach us to estimate them by the measure of our own.'

Hastings's views remained Eurocentric; he did not suggest that European and Indian civilizations were equal, and it would be surprising in the cultural context of the eighteenth century if he had. But he did believe that Indian civilization was right for India, a sensible pragmatism if nothing else, but one which was to be abandoned in the nineteenth century and under attack before his death. He saw the new British empire in India as displaying the tolerance of the old Roman empire in the west. As early as 1763 he had written that the 'wisest and most permanent states have ever left to conquered nations the exercise of their own laws'. The later men of the Indian empire were not to think of themselves as Romans but as the superior Guardians of the Greek, Plato.

The most common – and the harshest – verdict history can hand down on men and events is silence. After all the fanfaronade, the fear and the hatred the nabobs inspired in the entrenched establishment, what is left? The empire of which they were the unwitting progenitors has gone for ever. We can still, by courtesy of the National Trust, visit some of their great houses, but few know or care from where the money came that built them. A whiff of sulphur may still cling to the satirical cartoons that attacked the nabobs with a viciousness that makes today's efforts almost anodyne by comparison, but it is now more likely to cause laughter than the choke of anger. In literature the half-life of the nabob lasted until the middle of the nineteenth century, by way of the essays of Macaulay to the novels of Benjamin Disraeli and William Makepeace Thackeray. 'Isn't he very rich?' asks Rebecca in the latter's *Vanity Fair* and receives the reply 'They say all Indian Nabobs are enormously rich'. Like all epitaphs, it does not tell the whole truth.

Index

Afghans, 18, 73
Ahmad Shah Abdali, 73
Alexander, Claud, 179
Alipur: Hastings' duel at, 116;
   Hastings' house and garden
   at, 94, 181
Alivardi Khan, Nawab, 20
Allahabad, 73, 74, 75, 78–9, 87
American War of Independence,
   59, 106–7, 124, 143, 152, 175
Asaf-ud-Daulah, Nawab of
   Oudh, 125, 127, 130, 131,
   132-5; Hastings' treaty with
   (1781), 131, 133–4
Asiatic Society, 180
Aurangzeb, Emperor, 18

Baillie, Colonel, 122
Banaras, 27, 30, 39, 79, 80, 87,
   112, 125, 126, 128, 136, 146,
   158, 159, 180; Haidar Ali's
   insurrection (1781), 126–32,
   144, 145; Treaty of (1773), 78,
   86, 93
Banks, Thomas, 40
Barber, Sir Robert, 74, 76
Barwell, Richard, 38, 66, 68–9,
   71, 72, 84, 87, 88, 90–1, 92,
   95, 98, 99, 100, 101, 102–5,
   106, 108, 109, 110, 112, 131,
   141, 145

Basildon Park, Berkshire, 38
Beckford, Alderman William,
   54–5
Begums of Oudh, 133–5, 159–
   60, 163, 164, 167, 170, 171
Benfield, Paul, 37
Bengal Club, 52
Bengal Council, 64, 66–73, 86–
   104 *passim*, 106, 108–9, 112–
   13, 114, 115, 117, 120, 123,
   125, 126, 131, 139, 140, 142,
   145, 146–7, 148, 174, 175
Berar, Raja of, 125, 130
Berkeley Square, Clive's house
   in, 34, 45
Bhagavad-gita, Wilkins'
   translation of, 180–1
bills of exchange, 30–1, 177
Board of Revenue, 102, 115,
   146, 174
Bogle, George, 181
Bombay, 17, 18, 51, 64, 108,
   109, 111, 137
Boswell, James, 14
Bristow, John, 86, 99, 106, 110,
   117, 136, 144, 145, 146
Brown, Lancelot 'Capability', 35
Browne, Major James, 147–8
Burdwan, Rani of, 88–9, 92
Burgoyne, General John, 59, 61,
   62, 63, 106–7, 152

185